Thrive Not Just Survive

How To Live From Within

D. Scott Cook

TWS Publishing

Copyright © 2025 by D. Scott Cook

All rights reserved.

Published by TWS Publishing
Lodi, CA
www.thewriterssociety.online

No part of this publication may be reproduced, stored in a retrieval system, transmitted in any form or by any means — electronic, mechanical, digital, photocopy, recording, or any other (except for brief accredited quotations in printed reviews) without the publisher's prior permission.

NO AI TRAINING: Without in any way limiting the author's [and publisher's] exclusive rights under copyright, any use of this publication to train generative artificial intelligence (AI) technologies to generate text is expressly prohibited. The author reserves all rights to license uses of this work for generative AI training and development of machine learning language models.

The author of this book does not dispense medical advice or prescribe the use of any technique as a form of treatment for physical, emotional, or medical problems without the advice of a physician, either directly or indirectly. The intent of the author is only to offer information of a general nature to help you in your quest for emotional and spiritual well-being. In the event you use any of the information in this book for yourself, the author and the publisher assume no responsibility for your actions.

Scripture quotations marked ESV are taken from the ESV® Bible (The Holy Bible, English Standard Version®), copyright © 2001 by Crossway, a publishing ministry of Good News Publishers. Used by permission. All rights reserved.

Scripture quotations marked NET are from the NET Bible® copyright ©1996, 2019 by Biblical Studies Press, L.L.C. http://netbible.com. All rights reserved.

All Scripture marked with the designation "GW" is taken from GOD'S WORD®. © 1995, 2003, 2013, 2014, 2019, 2020 by God's Word to the Nations Mission Society. Used by permission.

Scripture taken from the New King James Version® marked NKJV. Copyright © 1982 by Thomas Nelson. Used by permission. All rights reserved.

Scripture quotations marked (NLT) are taken from the Holy Bible, New Living Translation, copyright © 1996, 2004, 2015 by Tyndale House Foundation. Used by permission of Tyndale House Publishers, Carol Stream, Illinois 60188. All rights reserved.

Scripture quotations taken from the New American Standard Bible®, Copyright © 1960, 1962, 1963, 1968, 1971, 1972, 1973, 1975, 1977, 1995 by The Lockman Foundation. Used by permission. All rights reserved. www.lockman.org

Scripture quotations taken from the Amplified® Bible (AMPC), Copyright © 1954, 1958, 1962, 1964, 1965, 1987 by The Lockman Foundation. Used by permission. All rights reserved. www.lockman.org.

Note: The author adds all italicized emphasis in Scripture quotations.

This book includes stories in which people's names and some details of their situations have been changed.

All internal art is produced by the author of the book.

Library of Congress Cataloging-in-Publication Data is available upon request.

PAPERBACK: ISBN 978-1-961180-95-6

KINDLE: ISBN 978-1-961180-96-3

HARDCOVER: ISBN 978-1-966818-05-2

To Jordan and Josh, I love you.

Contents

Preface ... ix
Introduction ... xi

Part One
A New Paradigm

1. Deconstructing Beliefs that Hold You Back ... 3
2. Changing Your Perspective ... 15
3. A Quantum Leap ... 25
4. Consciousness and Possibilities ... 39

Part Two
How It Works

5. Attention and the Power of Focus ... 57
6. Intention, Imagination, and Vision ... 65
7. The High Energy of Gratitude ... 75
8. The Power of Thoughts and Words ... 85
9. Manifesting in the Five Percent ... 97

Part Three
Live from Within: The Transition

10. Everything You Need Is Within You ... 113
11. Living from Within ... 127
12. Engaging Your Higher Self ... 141
13. Contemplation: The Key to Manifesting ... 151

Conclusion	171
Appendix One: Meditation Practices	185
Appendix Two: Contemplation Instructions and Template	189
Appendix Three: Affirmations	191
Notes	197
Acknowledgments	203
About the Author	205
Other Books by D. Scott Cook	207
Meet TWS Publishing	209

Preface

This is the last of three books that, taken together, lead the reader through the process of inner healing, transitioning from controlling religion to a spirituality they can embrace, and finally, learn to live from within so you can thrive, not just survive.

This is the culmination of a dramatic change in focus and beliefs. I spent most of my life learning theology, studying, and applying scripture. To me, the Bible was the Word of God and our focus in life.

But in 2004, God began a process of deconstructing my theology, view of the Bible, and worldview. *Sidetracked in The Wilderness* by Michael Wells made the point that God did not send us a book; He sent us a baby who became a Man. The Shepherds did not go to Mary and Joseph in the stable to see a book; they went to see a baby, the Messiah, who was Christ the Lord. He is our focus, not a book. The Bible supports Christ. It is His servant, not His master. Nor ours.

God opened my mind to "general" revelation, His creation. I began to see things from a new perspective through quantum physics. I studied the testimony of those who had near-death experiences and returned to give witness to what they saw and how it changed their lives. I studied astronomy and saw that His universe is indescribably vast and billions of years old. I studied anthropology, humanity's beginnings, and the migrations that occurred and affected history over many years. This included examining the mimetic theory of Rene Girard,[1] the French sociologist and anthropologist, which challenged my understanding of Christ's atonement through the scapegoat mechanism[2] we see in human history.

All of this began a process of deconstructing what I had been taught about the Bible: salvation, atonement, the character of God, and living spiritually versus religiously. It allowed me to reconstruct a spiritually Christo-centric theology, open to general revelation rather than a theology confined to a book from a certain religious, denominational orientation.

I am thankful to every person who has instructed me along the journey. People like Steve McVey, Francois duToit, Andre Rabe, Paul Young, Rene Girard, David Bentley Hart, Michael Wells, John Crowder, Fred Alan Wolf, Bruce Rosenblum, Fred Kuttner and many others. Some of whom I know, others I have never met but have benefited dramatically from their books and online resources. From theology to philosophy, psychology, anthropology, sociology, quantum physics, and astronomy, each discipline helped me write this book.

As you learn to live from an inner life of spirit rather than an outward material focus, I believe you will enjoy being your authentic self. Not the false persona I and others call the "ego" or what the Apostle Paul calls the "flesh." The true you in soul focused on your essence as a spirit, one in Christ's (the Source, or Light) Spirit, the way He intended you to live and manifest. If this book helps you on this journey, even a little, it will have fulfilled its purpose.

Introduction

My brother asked me to go to lunch one day to discuss something he was excited about. When I sat down at the restaurant with him, he began to talk about a book that had opened his mind to the reality of quantum physics. He was fascinated by the potential application to our daily lives and how it had already affected him. What excited him was the application to believers in Christ and how they approach spirituality and religion. I had been introduced to the realities of quantum physics six months earlier and shared his excitement. We were both heading in a common direction and did not know it.

I see a new reformation taking place, and many people are participating but do not know it yet. This introduction to quantum physics was partly responsible for deconstructing my theology as a former evangelical Southern Baptist seminary graduate and pastor. I began to see God's creation and myself in a new light based on His creative genius and pattern. God's general revelation (we will discuss this in more detail in chapter two) in quantum physics would be the starting place to lead me into greater awareness and revelation of all God had done in Christ that was so much bigger than my limited theological beliefs and understanding.

If you believe God is not good and perfect love, then your relationship with the Divine will suffer, and loving yourself and others is incredibly difficult. If you do not know your true identity in Him, you will work to build an identity, a false persona, based on your work and efforts rather than your life in Him. Loving others comes when you know your identity and love whom God made you in His image and likeness. People are not out or in; they are one in Christ (the Divine Life), one with you. To love your neighbor is to love Christ and yourself.

Thrive Not Just Survive: How to Live From Within is the journey from living in a predetermined theological and psychological religious construct that keeps you focused outwardly, to living in the reality of a loving God, who cannot be put in a box, and Christ Jesus (the Divine incarnate) in whom everything finds its meaning. This frees you to live inwardly in spirit rather than outwardly focused on material things, which are temporal and irrelevant to inner peace and rest. This means coming into the awareness and revelation of what already is in Christ, not what can be. Instead of 'building the kingdom," you go inward to a spiritual kingdom that encompasses everything and is complete in Christ.

Everything I was taught in the church had to do with an external focus; even prayer became an external exercise right down to kneeling when you prayed and how you prayed. Everything was scripted and rehearsed rather than organic, spontaneous, and natural. It felt fake because it was fake. Bible reading became a set time in the morning to ensure you started your day with scripture. Giving was based on 10 percent of everything you ever made, or God would not bless you. Never mind that giving is a spontaneous reaction to internal love that affects external behavior. Witnessing became a sales mission, convincing as many people as possible that you were right about Jesus, salvation, hell, and living a good life. Constant expansion of the church's property with new buildings, more people attending, and serving in the many programs the church offered. None of it led to the inner life of the person's soul and their true essence in spirit. None of it could heal the internal emotional wounds of the past, nor tear down and replace the false identities that dominate each person. And the worst part, those who sought a different direction of the inner spirit were ridiculed and dismissed as too heavenly-minded to be of any earthly good.

The inner life of most Christians is so underdeveloped that even discussing this in a pulpit would leave most confused or ambivalent. Many pastors are ill-equipped to minister to their flocks spiritually. Instead, they focus on building an organization, convincing people to give, and preaching motivational sermons that give steps or principles to follow. Not only is this not reflective of who Jesus was and what He taught in His ministry on Earth, but it is not what the church was called to be. The church is a spiritual body of people who have responded to the call of the inner spirit.

> *For we are the circumcision, who worship by the Spirit of God and glory in Christ Jesus and put no confidence in the flesh.*
> Philippians 3:3 ESV

This focus on outward material things has created a pseudo-community of people who do not know the difference between their inner life of the Spirit and the external manifestation of that life.

I am not advocating for the use of gifts of the Spirit and the expression of those gifts, whether tongues, prophecy, healing, mercy, or others. All spiritual gifts are proper and beneficial for blessing others when applied in and by the Holy Spirit. This book focuses on the authentic you in the soul, your essence in spirit, and living from that essence.

The book has three parts. Part one focuses on letting go of the old so you can receive the new and live from within. We will examine the importance of deconstructing theology and doctrines that have held you back from living in the reality of a loving and good God and considering specific and general revelation. This deconstruction and reconstruction can be a little difficult and scary, but it is necessary to live from your spirit and the soul rest and peace that is yours in Christ. The importance of specific and general revelation from a balanced perspective is also looked at. Through the ages, many theologians and church leaders have focused on special revelation to the exclusion of general revelation. Science and the growth of technology have expanded our understanding of the universe God created allowing us a more balanced approach to interpret scripture and develop our theological beliefs. In the last two chapters of Part one we will look at quantum physics and what it says about how God's universe works at the most smallest possible level. For years christians have focused strictly on the Bible to the exclusion of what God has revealed in quantum physics and other areas of study such as anthropology, astronomy, and geology. While specific revelation has its place, it is incomplete without respect for God's general revelation. So much has been revealed over the last 150 years, and much more is being revealed daily. In a few years, quantum computing, with its speed and efficiency, will make personal computers irrelevant. This technological breakthrough alone will open never-before-seen opportunities to receive a greater revelation of God's beautiful universe and its many facets. [1]

Part two looks at how creation functions versus what we have been taught in religious dogma. Focus and being in the moment determine outcomes and the use of your imagination to see what God sees in the endless possibilities of the kingdom in Christ.

We will examine emotions as the energy that attracts like-energy to you. How emotions such as gratitude, thanksgiving, and joy align with faith— seeing Christ's completed work on your behalf in and with you. Chapter eight examines explicitly the importance of our thoughts and what we say. Thoughts and words are energy with unique frequencies and amplitudes which attract similar energy and frequencies based on that energy (this is not pseudo-science; this has been tested in experiments and proven true, as we will see). Knowing what we are saying is as important as what we say. Many are conditioned to speak lies to themselves, and it is an unconscious habit that hurts them and those they love. Changing that and directing it along God's grace and love for you is possible.

We will finish part two by seeing how every action has an equal and opposite reaction. Manifestations start from what you focus on, intend, feel, and confess. These habits learned over a lifetime impact your life direction. It is easier to complain about life than to do something different based on how God created the universe to operate and Jesus' instructions on participating in His creation.

Part three looks at this inner life focus from a practical standpoint: What does living inside-out actually look like? How does it work? It is essential to release the religious and cultural hang-ups that keep us in a rut. Religion demands time, energy, and loyalty to dogma and the tribe. This culture demands an outward focus on material things and achievement versus a focus on our inner life of soul and spirit.

The reality is that everything you need is within you in your union with the Spirit of Christ Jesus. Part three also looks at the soul focused outward instead of inward on the Spirit and alignment of spirit, soul, and body working together in unity. The challenge of transitioning from an outward-focused life to an inward focus on the Spirit is examined.. The gravitational forces that keep us focused outwardly can be challenging to break, but every person can live from their essence in spirit. The last chapter, notably, explores living by Spirit in the moment. Living in the moment (mindfulness) brings our attention to the inner Spirit, and contemplation allows us to listen to the Spirit in silence. Rethinking what prayer is and how we transition from talking to listening through contemplation is fundamental to thriving.. This transition from our efforts to being in the moment and listening is essential to live from the inside out and be our authentic selves.

The book's end contains three appendices: Meditation practices to help you begin meditating, Contemplation aids to help you develop your contemplative practice, and I AM affirmations for daily use.. All of these will be helpful as you begin this journey of the inward way.

Finally, I hope you come to this book with an open mind and a ready heart to listen. I do not expect everyone to agree with all my viewpoints and theological beliefs. I only ask one thing: Would you ask the Spirit within you, "How does it apply to me?" If you are still uncomfortable, then move in another direction. I have found that when people are open and available to learn and grow, these truths are easier to digest and benefit from.

I do critique some beliefs and traditions you may hold. I do not intend to attack anyone or put anyone down based on their beliefs. I respect your right to believe as you choose. But if this book is in your hands, it is there for a purpose, and the Source of all life is interested in saying something to you through it.

Join me on the journey of living from within, the true you, and begin to thrive, not just survive!

Part One

A New Paradigm

Chapter 1

Deconstructing Beliefs that Hold You Back

The illiterate of the 21st Century will not be those who cannot read and write, but those who cannot learn, unlearn and relearn.

Alvin Toffler

During the summer before my senior year in high school, I worked for a private construction contractor demolishing some walls and flooring in a school to make way for a new atrium near the entrance. The area we were working on was a classroom used for English classes. It was in perfect shape; the paint looked great, the flooring was cared for, and the lighting worked well. The electricity in the room was working, and all the plugs had an electrical current. There was a closet with plenty of storage space and shelves for supplies. There were whiteboards on two walls and a screen to show movies or transparencies on an overhead projector. Everything was in good working order for the next English class in the fall semester. Except for one thing. That space was needed for a higher function: a new atrium, which would allow effortless traffic flow for more students. The school was rapidly growing, and the atrium was essential for servicing the number of students in attendance. It would also create a welcoming area for new students and parents who came to the school. So, while English is essential and needs a classroom to be taught, the atrium was the next step in the growth and development of the school.

This is like your spiritual journey. The religious room you are living in and using seems excellent. The paint is in good shape, and the floors are sound and polished. The whiteboards are in working order, and there is a great closet for everything you need to store. Except for one thing.

There is a greater purpose, and that room is no longer big enough or functional to serve the next step on your journey. The room must be deconstructed and reconstructed if you want to grow in greater spiritual awareness and live from your inner spirit. This begins by examining our religious group and the beliefs that may hold us back.

For those who did not grow up in or with religion, or are currently not practicing Christianity, this section is likely immaterial to you. Feel free to skip it and chapter two and move to chapter three. For those who grew up in Christianity, please continue.

Your Religious Group Is a Small Minority

According to the Center for the Study of Global Christianity, Gordon-Conwell Theological Seminary, there are over 2.3 billion Christians today.[1] This number is broken up into smaller groups, as shown on the pie chart in Figure 1.1.

Catholics comprise the most at 35 percent, while Mainline Protestants and Pentecostals-Charismatics each comprise over 18 percent of Christians worldwide. Evangelicals are 11 percent, while Eastern Orthodox are 7 percent. The remainder is a mix of unaffiliated and non-denominational groups.

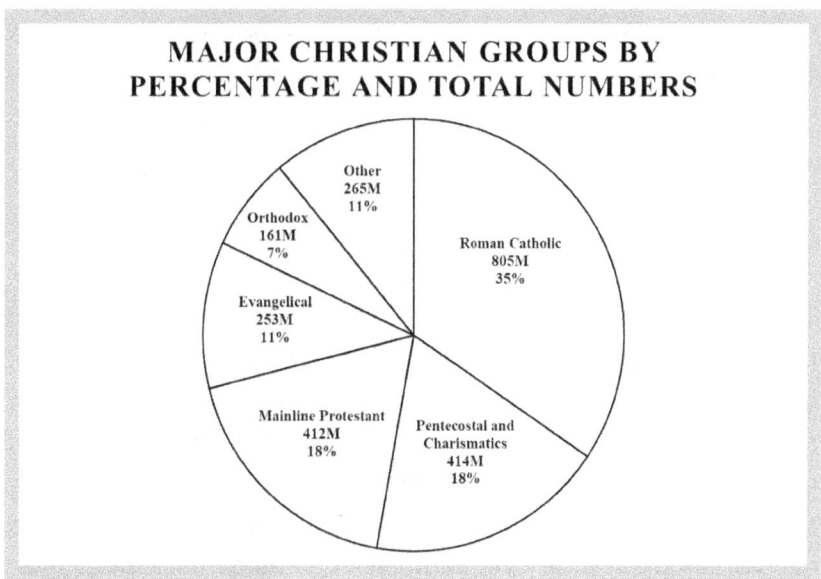

Figure 1.1 Christianity has over 2.3 billion adherents worldwide, roughly 30 percent of the world's population. However, it is divided and fragmented, with over 45,000 denominations across five major groups.[2]

As mentioned, I grew up in and pastored Southern Baptist churches. I thought my specific denomination was the whole world. I read their materials, listened to their pastors and leaders, and lived in a religious bubble. I knew many other denominations did not believe as we did, but I was unwilling to consider what others believed or taught for fear of being misled; my group was correct in our theology, not theirs. Yet Southern Baptists only number around 14 million today. Based on the numbers we just reviewed, my former denomination represents 0.59 of one percent of all Christianity. It takes a sizable amount of pride to believe you have all the truth and that everyone else is wrong when you make up less than 1 percent of all Christians worldwide. But that is the Christian denominational world. If there are over 45,000 denominations in five very different groups, how could your small group within Christianity hold all the truth? Ask yourself, "Have I ever considered that my small denominational group does not hold ALL the truth?"

Your Denomination Does Not Hold the Keys to the Truth

This is difficult to hear, but your small denomination (including Catholics who are also divided in theological views within the church), be it Southern Baptist, Presbyterian, Charismatic, Pentecostal, Evangelical Free Church, or whomever you are associated with, does not have a monopoly on truth. They may have some things completely wrong, some partially correct, and others correct. Unfortunately, some teachings are based on centuries of tradition rather than a dynamic theology and a willingness to change and grow spiritually. Theology is not static, and God cannot be put into a theological box, no matter how often your pastor told you, "All revelation is final." The reformers' beliefs were not entirely those of the Council of Nicaea in 325 C.E. They varied. The opinions of many Pentecostals differ from those of Martin Luther, and the same can be said for Southern Baptists.

A willingness to examine your theology and doctrine, with an open mind and heart to the leading of the Spirit within you, is a sign of spiritual growth and maturity. An unwillingness to do so is a sign of spiritual immaturity. It is also acquiescing to the internal control of fear rather than the freedom that comes from knowing you are loved unconditionally by God above all else. I do not say this to criticize anyone. It is simply a fact. The Apostle Paul wrote,

> *But I, brothers, could not address you as spiritual people, but as people of the flesh, as infants in Christ. I fed you with milk, not*

> *solid food, for you were not ready for it. And even now you are not yet ready.*
> I Corinthians 3:1-2 ESV

> *The natural person does not accept the things of the Spirit of God, for they are folly to him, and he is not able to understand them because they are spiritually discerned. The spiritual person judges all things but is himself to be judged by no one.*
> I Corinthians 2:14-15 ESV

Let the Spirit who lives within you be your guide to teach, instruct, and awaken you to truths you have been unaware of. Let Him reveal how to apply them. Then, in your union in Christ, work with Him to decipher what He is developing within you so that you may live at a higher level of consciousness in Him each moment.

I do not claim to have all the answers. But I am growing in greater awareness of what I was unaware of yesterday, a greater revelation from the Holy Spirit and how it applies to me, and then working it out practically in union with Christ to live at a higher level of consciousness. That is the true definition of spiritual maturity. You need not be afraid of being misled. Look to the Spirit who lives within you to be your guide. He will keep you from errors while you grow.

What Is Theological Deconstruction?

Theological deconstruction is an approach to religious beliefs that seeks to break down the various interpretations of a given faith tradition to understand how each opinion is constructed. It examines how specific doctrinal statements are understood and used by adherents of the Christian faith, focusing on deconstructing specific ideas about God, the Bible, salvation, etc.

By breaking down these ideas, theological deconstruction allows us to question what these concepts mean and how they apply to our lives. It also allows us to explore the various implications of these interpretations and why they impact us.

The aim of theological deconstruction is to arrive at *a more honest appreciation of religious faith*. This honesty can be liberating, as individuals are no longer required to accept the traditional interpretations of their faith without question or negotiation. Through deconstruction, we can arrive at a more honest, fuller understanding of our faith.

Theological deconstruction does not necessarily invalidate Christianity's interpretation of scripture or traditions. Rather, it encourages us to think more openly about faith. It takes on a critical role, inviting believers to become more engaged with why we believe what we believe.

Theological deconstruction is not a casual endeavor. It requires substantial, thoughtful engagement and effort. It is an ongoing process that asks us to be open to new ideas and interpretations of our faith. It can open new possibilities for believers, allowing for more understanding and light on our faith walk with Christ.

The Benefits of Theological Deconstruction

I remember being in churches where the pastors encouraged us to have a faith that is ours, not our parents. This means we must come to the point that what we believe is based on our own research, study, and conviction, not because someone told us to believe it. The same holds for us today.

Why do you believe what you believe? For most, it is because our pastor taught it, our parents believed it, or we heard it from a youth minister. But why do you believe it? Did you experience it with God? Or do you hold to this theology because your religious tribe, family, or friends do?

Theological deconstruction is essential because you will struggle to move beyond a focus on the material world (made of matter and mass) without it. You will live based on what is temporal versus what is eternal. Temporal things are what you can see, hold, and touch. They are material in nature and, therefore, temporary. It is the unseen world of spirit that is unending.

We don't look for things that can be seen but for things that can't be seen. Things that can be seen are only temporary. But things that can't be seen last forever.
II Corinthians 4:18 GW

Spirit looks to the unseen, the eternal, and the actual Reality (temporal material things are also real, but with a small "r." Spirit is Reality, big R, as all things have come from the unseen spirit world. We will look at this in detail in later chapters). By being more open, we become more teachable and can grow in our awareness, the revelation of how to apply it, and higher consciousness, living out each moment in spirit. When we know God loves us and that He can be trusted, we trust He will lead us into all truth by His Spirit[3] , which is one with us. Then, we are empowered to operate as spiritual people and discern matters through spiritual means.

Theology and doctrine are fluid, vibrant, and changing—not because God changes but because we become more aware. It is like a mist that slowly lifts, and we can see a little further than we could earlier. The Spirit is the one who raises the mist. *But fear of change, being deceived, or being rejected by our religious group keeps us in the mist.* Growing spiritually required me to allow my fears to fall to the One who loves me unconditionally. When I began to experience His unconditional love for me, I no longer feared being deceived, led astray, changing, or even rejected by family, friends, and those at church. To grow spiritually is to grow out of one thing and into something more significant once we know it. I encourage you to read chapter ten of my book *Alignment of Authentic Love* to learn more about this process of having our beliefs pruned and new ones grown in their place to bear fruit. God loves you; you can trust Him. The Spirit lives in you and will keep you from error. Be assured. If your friends reject you because of your spiritual growth, God will bring new friends who will rejoice with you in the new thing He is doing in your life.

The Necessity of Theological Reconstruction

Once a house or building has been torn down, the area is cleared to prepare for a new structure. Sometimes, the old foundation can be used again; other times, it must be removed. Reconstruction requires preparing the lot to build the new structure.

The same is true for reconstructing our theology after we have spent some time deconstructing it. A warning: This must be done with the Spirit, based on His timing and method. If you are ready, you will know it. If you are not, you will know that too. There is no hurry. Wait on God's timing and allow Him to determine the method and pace of the journey.

An example of this is seen in the life of the Apostle Paul. After his Damascus Road experience, the Spirit revealed to him that his theology and zeal for God were misplaced and wrong. He spent three days, blind and unwilling to eat, as he came to terms with the reality that what he thought was true was not. Jesus Christ was the Messiah; Jewish people following Him were doing God's will, and his persecution of them was literally persecuting God. As someone who was raised a Pharisee (one of the religious sects that led Judaism in that day), knew the Mosaic law, and had a zeal for it and his country, it was a devastating revelation. It brought his entire life crumbling to his feet and begged the question: What is the truth, and how was I so wrong?

This is similar to what many of us have gone through in deconstructing our theology. We have the Damascus Road experience; our eyes are opened, and we see from a new and different perspective. And we, too, ask: What is the truth, and how was I so wrong? This is the most wonderful place because it is the start of something new that will bring you somewhere you have never been before, theologically, emotionally, and spiritually.

But once the deconstruction begins and we tear down the old façade of religion and self-righteousness, we must cooperate with the Spirit to reconstruct a new foundation on our union in Christ and God's unconditional love. Paul did this by leaving Damascus and going to Arabia, which would have been a four-week walk on foot. Unfortunately, I do not think this verse is well understood among evangelicals.

> *For you have heard of my former way of life in Judaism, how I was savagely persecuting the church of God and trying to destroy it. I was advancing in Judaism beyond many of my contemporaries in my nation, and was extremely zealous for the traditions of my ancestors. But when the one who set me apart from birth and called me by his grace was pleased* (to reveal his Son in me) *so that I could preach him among* (in) *the Gentiles, I did not go to ask advice from any human being, nor did I go up to Jerusalem to see those who were apostles before me, but right away I departed to Arabia, and then returned to Damascus. Then after three years I went up to Jerusalem to visit Cephas and get information from him, and I stayed with him fifteen days. But I saw none of the other apostles except James the Lord's brother.*
> Galatians 1:13-19 NET

God set Paul apart for a particular purpose, called him to that purpose, and revealed that Christ lived within him, not just outside him or through temple rituals. He did not have Christ in him because of a prayer he prayed, a commitment he made, or sincerely repenting of his sins. That is where Christ always was, and Paul was always in Christ, as all things are in Christ. And this life that lived in Paul, in the person of Jesus Christ, was the truth about him. All of this was God's doing. None of it was Paul's. And it destroyed the foundation of everything Paul stood on regarding the old covenant law.

Paul did something spiritual: He did not seek the advice of those in Damascus or go back to Jerusalem to talk to the Jewish religious rulers or the apostles. Why? Christ lived in him. He did not need their counsel. Paul was one with God in Christ. All he needed was within him by the Spirit. God revealed to him what already existed: Christ in him, the Source of everything.

He stayed in Arabia for some time, but we do not know how long. I suspect that it was longer than two years. Deconstruction and reconstruction can take some time, and it is the work of the Spirit to reveal what is needed and when. You and I cannot handle everything at once, and it is better to be given something according to our ability to receive and process it. To do this, Paul needed to escape from everyone and everything that had anything to do with Judaism or Christianity. Be quiet and let the Holy Spirit do the inner work in His time and His way. No crusades, no witnessing, no appeals for money, no starting new churches, no results of any kind. Just listening to the Spirit who lived within him and with whom he was one—listening with spiritual knowing and intuition to the voice of the inner Spirit. Reconstruction comes as we learn to be quiet, to stop struggling and striving, or working and doing, and to be still and listen.

In my theological deconstruction and reconstruction, I realized that I needed to escape everything that held me to the past, from everyone and everything in institutional organized Christianity. To be quiet, listen to the spirit, and do nothing of value materially but of immense value spiritually. Just listen without striving or judging. Instead, I enjoyed each moment as it came to me. There is no agenda, no work, just the presence of Christ in me and me in Him. True Reality. This did more for my spiritual growth, spiritual awareness, and living from within.

Paul eventually returned to Damascus and, three years later, went to Jerusalem. But even then, it was by spiritual intuition, not his effort or plans. He would never again be tied to a movement, a religion, or religious legalistic people-pleasing. His very life was Christ (Colossians 3:3, 4; Philippians 1:21). Not working for Christ, witnessing for Christ, sharing Christ, or starting churches for Christ. No, his very life was Christ Himself. Christ in him, He in Christ: Union. No separation and no duality. His theological deconstruction and reconstruction resulted in one thing, or Person if you will: Christ. No longer Paul and his legalism, knowledge, doing, or past. Just Christ.

This is what deconstruction and reconstruction should do: Leave you with nothing but Jesus (the Divine Life) and the unconditional love of God that has no expectations or exceptions. I pray that you not only enter this with God in spirit but also learn to let go of control and enjoy the journey into the true Reality. Christ is in you, and you in Christ.

Chapter 2

Changing Your Perspective

You cannot speak of the ocean to a frog that lives in a well.

Bill Vaughan

"The Allegory of the Cave" is a philosophical tale by the ancient Greek philosopher, Plato. In this story, Plato describes a group of men chained inside a dark cave since childhood. They are facing a wall, and their bodies are restrained, so they cannot turn around and see what is behind them. Behind the men is a fire burning, and between the fire and the men, there are objects and people passing by. These objects cast shadows on the wall the men are facing, so the only reality the men know is that of the shadows. The men have been in this state for so long that they have accepted this shadowy reality as the only truth. They have created a language to describe the shadows, and they argue over their interpretations of the shadows, believing that they represent the ultimate truth.

One day, one man is freed from his chains and forced to turn around and face the fire. At first, he is dazzled by the brightness of the light and cannot see the objects causing the shadows. Slowly, he begins to see the objects and perceives they are the source of the shadows. He realizes his previous reality was nothing more than an illusion. The man returns to the cave to tell the others what he has discovered, but they do not believe him. They think he is crazy and refuse to listen to him. They prefer to remain in their comfortable ignorance rather than face the truth and all the challenges that come with it.

"The Allegory of the Cave" is a powerful metaphor for the human condition. It suggests that many of us live in ignorance and illusion, accepting what we see on the surface as the ultimate truth. But when we are exposed to new information, we can gain a new perspective and break free from the chains that bind us to ignorance.

Changing our perspective can be scary. When we believe one thing and something else might add to the truth of it, it causes us to doubt ourselves and possibly everything we have put our trust in. After thirty-five years of ministering to Christians, I have found that very few trust Christ Jesus. They say they do, but in reality, they trust what they can see, touch, and feel (such as preachers, theological belief systems, and religious institutions) more than Christ. It is a bit of a farce in some ways, but they are not cognate of it. It often takes a traumatic event to help them see reality. Then, they can see how big Christ is versus their small theology. In this chapter, we will look at what general and specific revelation are and why we need a balance of both to deconstruct our theology and reconstruct it properly.

Special Revelation and Religious Dogma

Special revelation refers to God's self-disclosure to individuals through miraculous events, dreams, visions, and the Bible. This type of revelation is distinct from general revelation, which refers to God's self-disclosure through nature and conscience.

One of the main weaknesses of special revelation is its subjectivity. Individuals can have different experiences and interpretations of what God is revealing to them. This subjectivity can lead to conflicts within the church, where one person's understanding of special revelation can conflict with another's. Another weakness of special revelation is that it can be misinterpreted. This misinterpretation can be harmful to individuals and the assembly.

Christianity's over-reliance on special revelation has led to a rigid dogmatism[1] and intolerance of differing viewpoints. This over-reliance on special revelation causes the belief that one's interpretation of the Bible and God's will is the only valid one, leading to a lack of openness to new ideas and perspectives. Furthermore, over-reliance on special revelation causes a devaluation of reason and critical thinking. Christians who overemphasize special revelation can reject scientific discoveries and the knowledge gained through rational thought. This rejection then creates an anti-intellectualism that can hinder the progress of society.

For Evangelical Christians, the Bible is the primary source of special revelation. However, over-reliance on the Bible can lead to a rigid interpretation that is resistant to change. The Bible's historical context, as well as its translation and interpretation, can be lost, leading to a narrow understanding of God's will and message. It can also lead to a material focus rather than a spiritual understanding that should be primary in any teaching. This issue has plagued Christianity since the second century: What is truth? What are we to believe in and stand on? What is our focus? The tradition of Christianity has been ancient writings (now considered scripture), writings of the early church fathers, and archeological evidence that supports the Bible. None of these lead to transformation through your life in Christ and Christ in you (they can be stepping stones, but not an end in themselves). Nor do they lead to the revelation of what Christ in you means, how to apply it each moment, or your higher spiritual consciousness in which to live one's life. Thus, Christian tradition does not lead to greater spiritual maturity, which is the goal of the Spirit.

General Revelation

In Christian theology, general revelation refers to the knowledge of God that can be gained through observation and study of the natural world, and through human reason and conscience. General revelation is seen as a means by which God reveals Himself to all people, regardless of their religious beliefs or cultural background. General revelation is often associated with the biblical passage in Romans 1:20, *Since the creation of the world God's invisible qualities – His eternal power and divine nature – have been clearly seen, being understood from what has been made, so that people are without excuse.* NIV

Most Evangelical theologians believe general revelation can lead people to an awareness of God's existence and character but is not sufficient for salvation (more on salvation in a later chapter), which they believe requires a personal response to the gospel message of Jesus Christ.

God can use anything to introduce someone to His finished work in Christ. He does not need a gospel message for that. Love is the gospel message; general revelation can sometimes express that love better than the spoken word. Maybe through a star-lit night, the wind blowing through the trees in the afternoon, or the mockingbird's call as the sun rises. On the other hand, it could simply be the warm handshake and smile of another person that lights up your day. All of these are part of the Divine's general revelation.

General revelation has been placed in the back seat to special revelation for thousands of years. Orthodox Christianity has given a nod to it but not embraced it as science and technology have rapidly advanced. This fear of what science and technology may discover and reveal causes religion to resist its truths and cling to traditions and theological dogmas. Both hinder our spiritual growth and appreciation for who God is and His revelation in the person of Jesus Christ.

Science and Technology Are Outpacing Religious Dogma

The James Webb telescope was deployed in the summer of 2022. Since then, the telescope has allowed us to look deeper into space (effectively looking back in time, as the light we see left their stars billions of years ago) using infrared light to determine the age of the galaxies, stars, and black holes. The Webb telescope has discovered galaxies that are 500 to 700 million years older than they should be based on current cosmological theory. Through this telescope, we have seen galaxies never recorded before. We have learned that the universe is so big and expanding so rapidly that, ultimately, in billions of years, you will not see the light from other galaxies due to their distance from the Milky Way.

Through research and study of astronomy, we have also learned that the universe is over 13.8 billion years old.[2] Our solar system is only one of billions within the Milky Way galaxy, and the universe has trillions of galaxies. All the sand on Earth is less than the number of stars in the known universe.[3] All of this is general revelation of who God is in His love, creativity, and power. Think of the enormity of God's universe and how small our problems really are, yet He knows about each one and cares about us as if we were the only humans on Earth!

Quantum physics has upended our understanding of reality (physics) and how we measure it. These discoveries teach the importance of consciousness and observation, that everything is made of energy, and that even the smallest amount of energy is extremely powerful.[4]

Anthropology and archeology have discovered that humans have lived on Earth for six million years, and homo sapiens have lived for 200,000.[5] Humans have been growing crops for less than 10,000 years, and before that, they were hunter-gatherers who roamed in tribes as they followed the food supply (even that is now being questioned). And, every people group had some deity they sacrificed to and worshiped.[6] The migration of human beings has impacted the growth of cultures, languages, development of nations, and conflicts between those nations. This larger narrative helps us understand the development of Israel as a nation and the Bible in general over thousands of years.

Technology is expanding so rapidly that information doubles roughly every two years or less. One hundred years ago, there were very few phones. Today, nearly half the people on the planet carry a cell phone in their pocket, and it holds all the world's knowledge through its ability to connect to the internet. With artificial intelligence (AI), nearly any question can be answered within seconds, a picture created within minutes, and an entire novel written in less than an hour.

While these areas of general revelation continue to grow, the modern church clings to a literal understanding of scripture rather than a spiritual one that brings more illumination of mind and peace of soul. And it clings to the inerrancy of scripture due to fear rather than enjoying the freedom of our spiritual inheritance in Christ.

No wonder the world has moved on from institutional Christianity and its endless fights, schisms, denominational politics, sexual scandals, and lust for money and political power. Rather than embracing general revelation, as everything has been spoken into being by God the Father through Christ, religion has sought to defend its dogmatism, denominational belief systems, and outside agencies, organizations, and political structures. Is it not time we open our eyes and see that God is not only doing a new thing, but the world is already more aware of it than Christianity?

The Balance of General and Special Revelation

I am not saying that we should abandon special revelation, such as the scriptures, Jesus, prophecies, miracles, and signs. But just as it is important not to abandon special revelation, it is essential that we do not drift from general revelation.

We must strike a balance between these two areas that have not been achieved in times past. General revelation must be given the respect and importance it deserves so that we may more clearly understand special revelation.

For instance, quantum physics reveals that the universe does not operate like general physics. Matter, at its most basic level of electrons and protons of an atom, responds to the attention of an observer (more on this in chapters three and four). This can help us understand Jesus' statement:

> *I can guarantee this truth: This is what will be done for someone who doesn't doubt but believes what he says will happen: He can say to this mountain, 'Be uprooted and thrown into the sea,' and it will be done for him. That's why I tell you to have faith that you have already received whatever you pray for, and it will be yours.*
> Mark 11:23, 24 GW

Christians have many interpretations of this one passage. However, it takes on a new meaning and significance if you look at what quantum physics has revealed (general revelation) in the last one hundred years. To focus on the mountain and say to it, "Be uprooted and removed into the sea," is Jesus' way of saying the thing you place your attention on and focus on; agreeing that it is already done is the thing that will manifest in time. Quantum physics agrees with this and has proven that we live in a participatory universe. Your participation ultimately impacts what is manifested in your life.

Science and spirituality are now able to work together. Just as special revelation is of God, all that we see in the universe has been created by God. The only thing that keeps us from enjoying this revelation is fear. Fear of being deceived, fear of something new outside our comfort zone, and fear of losing what we have. But none of these fears are grounded in facts or faith. God is not someone you can put limitations on. He cannot be controlled, and He is not limited by anyone's theological belief systems. So, is it not time we let go of our fears, embrace the love and security of a good and loving God, and trust Him to give us more excellent light and understanding than we have ever enjoyed?

A New Paradigm

There are two additional types of revelation: Progressive and Continuous. From a biblical perspective, progressive revelation refers to the concept that God gradually revealed Himself and His divine plan to humanity throughout history. It suggests that God's revelation unfolded progressively, starting with the early patriarchs and culminating in the person of Jesus Christ. The Old Testament lays the foundation, foreshadowing and anticipating the coming of the Messiah, while the New Testament reveals the fulfillment of those promises in Jesus. This gradual revelation allowed for a deeper understanding of God's character, His redemptive plan, and the nature of salvation. It demonstrates God's intentional and purposeful approach to guiding humanity toward His ultimate revelation in Jesus Christ.

Continuous or continuing revelation in Christianity refers to the belief that God continues to reveal Himself and His will to individuals and the Church throughout history. It is the idea that divine revelation did not cease with the completion of the biblical canon but remains ongoing. Proponents of this concept believe that God's guidance, insights, and new understandings can be received through prayer, the Holy Spirit, communal discernment, and the study of scripture.

Continuous revelation provides a deeper understanding and application of existing truths in light of changing contexts and challenges. It acknowledges that God's revelation is not limited to the past but is relevant and active in the present, guiding believers in their spiritual journey.

A new paradigm is needed: a balance of general and special revelation with an understanding that this revelation is progressive and continuous. Science and spirituality work together rather than against each other. Just as God revealed Himself progressively up to the coming of the Messiah in Jesus Christ, He continues to reveal Himself and the truth about our union in Christ. He gives us more excellent light and understanding as we can receive it.

Continuous revelation provides a natural evolution from a God of judgment, anger, and punishment to knowing God as perfect Love, Light, and Life—as a God who is not against you but for you, as a God who loves you unconditionally without expectations.[7]

This new paradigm requires us to look at some realities of how the universe works and how that interweaves with the message of the gospel and our life in Christ. Instead of clinging to old constructs and beliefs, we embrace continuous revelation as part of spiritual growth. The growth that leads to a greater understanding and consciousness in the spirit each moment.

Would you be open to changing your mind? To a greater understanding of God and you as seen in general revelation? Are you willing to expand your spiritual horizons and embrace the journey of new discovery? This book will help you in that process if you are willing!

Chapter 3

A Quantum Leap

Everything we call real is made of things that cannot be regarded as real.

Niels Bohr

"The Matrix" is a popular science fiction movie that tells an extraordinary story. It introduces us to Thomas Anderson, also known as Neo, a computer programmer who stumbles upon a world filled with mysteries. In this future, machines have taken over, and humans are trapped in a simulated reality called the Matrix. Neo's journey within this artificial construct mirrors some mind-boggling concepts studied in quantum physics.

Quantum physics is a branch of science that explores the fundamental building blocks of our universe and how they behave in surprising ways. Just like Neo discovers a world beyond what he thought was real, quantum physics reveals a reality that challenges our everyday understanding.

In "The Matrix," Neo gains incredible abilities, defying the laws of nature within this simulated world. Similarly, quantum physics uncovers astonishing phenomena, such as particles existing in multiple states simultaneously or mysteriously connected no matter the distance between them.

These mind-bending discoveries might initially feel overwhelming, but they are part of the exciting journey we are about to embark on.

Beyond the mind-bending science, the movie delves into profound questions that echo the uncertainties we encounter when studying quantum physics. Questions about what is real, the nature of our identity, and the influence of our choices on the world around us. It is natural to feel curiosity and trepidation when exploring these complex topics, but we will navigate them together, shedding light on their wonders.

So, as we venture forth, remember that this chapter is a gentle introduction to a few quantum physics concepts while seeing how scripture and Christ Himself confirm this reality. We take our time to unravel its mysteries, appreciating the beauty of the concepts.

Embrace your curiosity, and let us embark on this exhilarating journey of discovery, where the extraordinary meets the unknown, where science and spirituality come together in a perfect weave of beauty.

Everything we will look at was created by God the Father through Jesus Christ, which is general revelation. Together, we will uncover the awe-inspiring wonders of God's quantum physics and why they are important to living from within.

The Matrix and the Kingdom

Neo knew that the world he called reality was not the substance of reality. It was a computer program created by machines to allow machines to harvest energy from human beings. In essence, humans had become the slaves of the very machines they created. This Matrix, as they called it, was not reality.

> *While we do not look at the things which are seen, but at the things which are not seen. For the things which are seen are temporary, but the things which are not seen are eternal.*
> II Corinthians 4:18 NKJV

Put another way, our focus should be on the unseen spirit that is eternal, not physical matter that is temporal. The Matrix appeared to be the substance of reality, but it was actually a computer program.

The same can be said for this material world we live in. It appears to be the primary reality (the Matrix), but it is not.

What is unseen, the spirit, is the primary reality.

> *The Pharisees asked Jesus when the kingdom of God would come. He answered them, "People can't observe the coming of the kingdom of God. They can't say, 'Here it is!' or 'There it is!' You see, the kingdom of God is within you."*
> Luke 17:20, 21 GW

The Pharisees wanted an outward sign of the coming of God's Kingdom into the world. But that Kingdom was already in front of them and already within them in their spirit—that which is unseen.

They wanted something they could see, taste, and touch; something in material form. He offered Himself, but they rejected Him.

This physical world seems to be the true reality, which we perceive as concrete and trustworthy. But it is temporal and fading. The substance of reality is in the unseen spirit.

> *It is the Spirit who gives life; the flesh profits nothing. The words that I speak to you are spirit, and they are life.*
> John 6:63 NKJV

Let me rephrase this, "It is unseen spiritual life that is important, not the outer material world and your efforts. My words are of this unseen spiritual reality and are true life." The material world seems to be the real substance of things, but it is not. Most people never understand that what they can see, taste, and touch is not the substance of reality. The Kingdom of God is bigger than matter or what you can see. It is within you and all around you. And all of it, including matter, is in Christ.

> *He is before all things, and all things are held together in Him.*
> Colossians 1:17

Everything, matter or unseen spirit, is in Christ and held together by Him. We want to focus on this unseen world of spirit. Quantum physics, God's general revelation, gives us a better understanding of what this universe is made of: matter and the unseen reality that undergirds it.

$E=MC^2$: Everything Is Energy

Albert Einstein's formula for the theory of special relativity began with his burning curiosity, and to unravel the mysteries of the universe. In 1905, he had a groundbreaking revelation that changed the course of physics forever.

Einstein pondered a profound question: Are the laws of physics the same for everyone, regardless of their motion? He delved into the nature of light, which always travels at a constant speed. From this observation, he deduced that space and time must be flexible and can be affected by how fast an object moves.

This led Einstein to formulate his famous equation: $E=MC^2$. The equation reveals the connection between energy (E) and mass (m). It states that a small amount of mass can hold an immense amount of energy. Nuclear reactions demonstrate that mass can be converted into energy and vice versa.

Einstein's discovery revolutionized our understanding of the universe. It laid the groundwork for advancements in nuclear power and explained the immense energy locked within matter. His ideas still inspire scientists to push the boundaries of knowledge and deepen our comprehension of the cosmos.

Matter (mass) and energy are the same thing. Mass can be converted into energy and vice versa, which means everything you see, no matter how small or large, is, at its essence, energy. And a small amount of matter carries a large amount of energy.[1]

What you look at every day in your kitchen, den, car, at work, or at the grocery store is all made of energy. This energy, in its most minor component, is made of atoms. Each atom has neutrons, protons, and various shells of electrons. The neutrons and protons are in the middle of the atom, with different levels of electrons around that middle (nucleus).[2]

Jesus described the Father as energy,

> *Again the high priest asked Him, saying to Him, "Are You the Christ, the Son of the Blessed?" Jesus said, "I am. And you will see the Son of Man sitting at the right hand of the Power, and coming with the clouds of heaven."*
> Mark 14:61, 62 NKJV

The Greek word for Power in this verse is *dunamis* and could be translated as energy. Jesus, in trying to explain who He was and what His future held, chose to describe the Father as *the Source of energy*. He also described His position as being seated. When someone is sitting, the work is done. There is no need to add to it. God is the Source of all life. He is the energy that creates and gives manifestation to all things. The more we study quantum physics, the more scripture comes alive.

The Importance of Energy Vibrations

Each physical object of matter gives off a specific energy vibration (signature) based on density, temperature, and pressure. A solid piece of matter generally has a lower frequency at a microscopic level but a higher energy potential due to its mass density. Fluids have less density, more motion, and the potential for higher frequencies than solids. Gases have the greatest variety of frequencies. But each gives off a specific vibrational signature.[3]

All energy resonates with similar energy signatures or vibrations. A piece of matter with a low vibrational signature will resonate with another piece of matter that vibrates at that frequency. It will resonate with that vibration and intensity if it has a higher vibration.[4]

In other words, people with low vibrations resonate with others with that vibration. In my work as a spiritual coach, I have found that people with a higher vibration and energy intensity tend to attract people with that same vibration and energy intensity. Birds of a feather flock together, if you will.

Have you ever sensed that someone had a low vibe? You can feel it almost immediately when someone is depressed, down, or negative. That vibe comes with them. Or maybe someone has a high vibe. The person is confident, encouraging, and positive, and that is the vibe they give off.

As a leader of several churches and businesses, I have interviewed many job applicants. I sought out those with solid high vibes (not to be confused with extroverts versus introverts, which are behavior styles). I wanted to connect my high vibe with theirs and feel their confidence and positivity. I never hired those with low vibes because they were not a good match for me or my team.

What does any of this have to do with living a spiritual life? Everything! As we will see, at the most minor building blocks of reality is a world of energy and vibration that operates based on observation and intent, directly relating to living your life from the inside out.

Your neural system produces thoughts and emotions. Those thoughts and emotions are energy; they give off a vibrational signature and energy intensity. The vibrational signature you give off is the resonance you will attract.

For example, if you constantly speak negativity into your life, such as, "Things never work out for me," that is the vibrational signature you attract. It is a scientific fact that energy resonates with energy of the same vibration.

Most of us are entirely unaware of the words we speak and the emotions we feel. Yet we complain about life circumstances, why we do not have what we need, and doubt God even cares about our situation. We do not know that we create our reality at that moment based on the things we think, say, and feel.

Most clients I work with in spiritual coaching are unaware of their constant negative self-talk. Things like "Everything I try fails," "I will never find a spouse," "I will always struggle financially," "I cannot do anything right," "I am probably crazy," "Something is wrong with me," "Nothing ever works out for me." When this is what you think, say, or feel, the emotions such as desperation, anger, and resentment that come with these will resonate and attract the things that carry that same vibrational signature. Unsurprisingly, we continue to get the same results we have always gotten.

Study Jesus' statements. You will find He did not speak fear, self-loathing, or destructive statements about His situations.

The key is awareness, attention, and focus. We will look at how each contributes to our outcomes later in the book.

Entanglement and the Unified Field

To understand quantum entanglement, let us explore it from the perspective of unified field theory. Unified field theory aims to describe all the fundamental forces of nature in a single, unified framework. It suggests an underlying field, often called the "quantum field," that permeates space and time. As everything is energy, this unified field is also energy, or dark energy, as it cannot be seen.[5]

In this framework, particles are not seen as separate entities but as excitations (the act of making something vibrate) or disturbances in the quantum field. When two particles become entangled, their properties, such as their position, momentum, or spin, become correlated so that the state of one particle is linked to the state of the other, *regardless of the distance between them.*

This entanglement occurs due to the interactions between the particles within the quantum field. When particles interact, they exchange information, which can become entangled, leading to a correlated state.[6]

Importantly, quantum entanglement does not involve any physical connection between the particles in the traditional sense. Instead, *it arises from the interconnected nature of the quantum field itself.*

This means that even if vast distances separate the entangled particles, any changes to one particle will instantaneously affect the other, defying our intuition about classical physics.

All of this is God's general revelation about His creation. Everything is energy, and it is connected in the unified field. That field is the Spirit of Christ, which holds all things together. The scriptures support this by saying it a little differently.

> *For all things in heaven and on earth were created by him—all things, whether visible or invisible, whether thrones or dominions, whether principalities or powers—all things were created through him and for him. He himself is before all things and all things are held together in him.*
> Colossians 1:16, 17 NET
>
> *Everything is from Him and by Him and for Him.*
> Romans 11:36a GW

Everything is created through Christ and held together in Him. It is from Him, through Him, and for Him. Therefore, this unified field of energy is Him.

Can you see how scripture and science come alive when combining specific and general revelations?

Everything is energy, and that energy exists in a unified field. When two particles are entangled, the impact on one of them impacts the other, no matter how far apart they may be. This is so because all things are united in this field.

Union is the most crucial point: we in Christ, Christ in the Father, Christ in us.

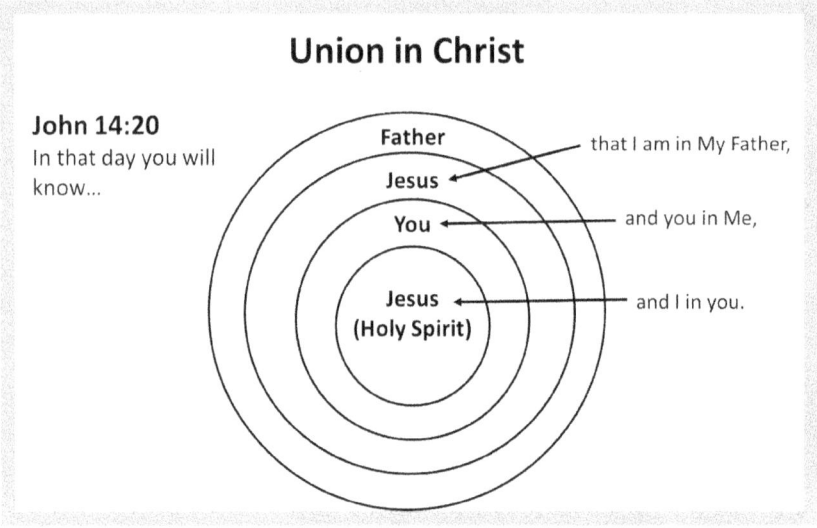

Figure 3.1 **As Christ is in the Father, we are in Christ, and Christ is in us. Christ is the unified field that holds all things together. We are one with Him as we are one with every person we will ever meet. We are one with all of creation in this field of energy.**

Living from within means living from your spirit, your essence. The Divine Life lives in you, is one with your spirit, and all you need lives within you. Science has confirmed what scripture taught us: all things are in union. Everything is in the Father, Christ is in the Father, we are in Christ, and Christ is in us. Living from within (your spirit) is natural. Living from the outside (your body, the world) to the inside is unnatural and creates problems. Focusing on outer material things such as people, money, relationship issues, possessions, power, position, and organizations will never bring inner peace and rest from which to live your highest life. Only by focusing inwardly on your spirit, where you are one with Christ and everything, can you do that.

Ninety-Five Percent of Everything

Matter is the stuff that makes up everything around us that we can see. It includes planets and stars, humans, plants, and animals. However, astonishingly, matter makes up only 5 percent of the total composition of the universe. So, what fills up the remaining 95 percent? Something scientists call dark matter and dark energy.

Dark matter makes up 27 percent of the known universe and is an invisible substance that cannot be seen or detected directly. Scientists infer its existence by studying its gravitational effects on visible matter. Dark matter's gravitational pull influences the movement of galaxies and holds them together. Although its exact nature remains unknown, it is thought to be made up of exotic particles that do not interact with light or other electromagnetic forces. While dark matter shapes the universe's structure, scientists are still trying to comprehend its true nature.

On the other hand, dark energy makes up 68 percent of the known universe and is a mysterious force that drives the universe's accelerated expansion. Unlike dark matter, dark energy does not clump together but instead fills up space uniformly. It seems to possess a repulsive property, pushing galaxies apart. Scientists believe that dark energy could be associated with the vacuum of space itself or *a form of energy that fills the cosmos.*

Dark matter and energy account for around 95 percent of the universe's composition. Understanding these forces is a captivating pursuit for scientists worldwide, as their exploration provides insights into the universe's fundamental nature and the forces that shape its evolution.[7]

Ninety-five percent of everything is unseen. Only 5 percent can be seen, felt, or handled, which is physical matter, primarily of solids, gases, and liquids. As we saw earlier in this chapter, the Apostle Paul wrote,

While we do not look at the things which are seen, but at the things which are not seen. For the things which are seen are temporary, but the things which are not seen are eternal.
II Corinthians 4:18 NKJV

It is the things of the spirit that matter most but cannot be seen, not the stuff of matter that can be seen. Even the universe cries out for our attention to the 95 percent, not the 5 percent. Yet we live our lives focused outside our spirit, on the things of matter. We see these things as being real and what life is about, yet they are not. It is your inner life that matters (no pun intended). Your inner spirit is one with Christ's spirit; in that union, you find your true identity and all that you need. We live from within first because our essence is spirit; it is the truth of who we are. As our soul focuses on our spirit, one with Christ, it manifests outwardly through the body into the world. In spirit, you are at peace, rest, and powerful. All that you need is and has always been within you.

A hundred years ago, quantum science began to show us a world within a world that we did not know or understand. If you asked Paul about molecules, atoms, and electrons, he would have stared at you. Why? Because he did not have the general revelation of God's creation in that area. What he knew was very surface, filled with myth and legend, and based on Jewish writings and history. But he did understand the importance of spirit, our oneness in Christ, and Christ's finished work that we are included in. That is why special revelation found in scripture and general revelation found in creation brings us a clearer picture of who God is, who we are, and who others are. Taken together, we can see the importance of living from our spirit and the difference it makes in our lives.

Chapter 4

Consciousness and Possibilities

It is often stated that of all the theories proposed in this century, the silliest is quantum theory. In fact, some say that the only thing that quantum theory has going for it is that it is unquestionably correct.

Michio Kaku

Consciousness is the remarkable ability to be aware of our surroundings, thoughts, and feelings and to reflect upon our existence. But hidden within this concept lies a world of endless possibilities waiting to be explored.

Imagine you possess a hidden key that unlocks the door to a world where the boundaries of reality are transcended. In this world, the power of your thoughts becomes a force of creation and exploration. With consciousness as your guide, you can shape the very fabric of existence, where ideas blossom into extraordinary journeys, and the seemingly impossible becomes within your reach.

Think of your mind as a vast landscape waiting to be discovered and molded. Like a skilled sculptor, you can mold your thoughts into intricate forms, giving life to new concepts and uncharted possibilities. Your mind becomes fertile ground where seeds of inspiration can take root and flourish, leading to discoveries and innovations that have the potential to change the world.

But consciousness is not only about personal exploration; it is a gateway to understanding and connection. Through consciousness, we gain insights into the thoughts and emotions of others, fostering empathy and compassion. It is a bridge that brings people together, promoting understanding and unity in a diverse and complex world.

Moreover, consciousness drives the engines of scientific progress and technological advancements. Like intrepid explorers, scientists utilize their consciousness to investigate the mysteries of the universe. They pose questions, conduct experiments, and analyze data, unlocking the secrets of nature and pushing the boundaries of human knowledge.

Through consciousness, we have unraveled the intricacies of DNA, ventured into the depths of space, and developed technologies that shape our daily lives.

Your consciousness is a precious gift. It holds the key to unexplored territories and limitless potential. Embrace the power of your imagination, curiosity, and critical thinking.

Let your consciousness be the guiding light that propels you toward a future filled with awe-inspiring accomplishments and boundless opportunities.

All Consciousness Is Non-Local

Non-local consciousness is the idea that our awareness and thoughts extend beyond our physical bodies and are not confined to a specific location.[1]

It suggests that consciousness is interconnected and can transcend the limitations of space and time. Scripture seems to agree that consciousness is non-local by the Spirit.

> *But Jesus, <u>knowing their thoughts</u>, said, "Why do you think evil in your hearts?"*
> Matthew 9:4 NKJV

> *Nathanael said to Him, "How do You know me?" Jesus answered and said to him, "Before Philip called you, when you were under the fig tree, <u>I saw you</u>."*
> John 1:48 NKJV

> *"I still have many things to say to you, but you cannot bear them now. However, when He, the Spirit of truth, has come, <u>He will guide you into all truth</u>; for He will not speak on His own authority, but whatever He hears He will speak; and <u>He will tell you things to come. He will glorify Me, for He will take of what is Mine and declare it to you.</u>*
> John 16:12-14 NKJV

> *For "who has known the mind of the LORD that he may instruct Him?" <u>But we have the mind of Christ.</u>*
> I Corinthians 2:16 NKJV

> *In the name of our Lord Jesus Christ, when you are gathered together, <u>along with my spirit</u>, with the power of our Lord Jesus Christ.*
> I Corinthians 5:4 NKJV

> *For though I am absent in the flesh, <u>yet I am with you in spirit</u>, rejoicing to see your good order and the steadfastness of your faith in Christ.*
> Colossians 2:5 NKJV

All consciousness is in Christ. The Spirit of Christ is what scientists call the unified field of energy that everything is connected to. The brain is a receiver, processor, and memory storage. The brain at work is the mind. Your volition, feelings, and thinking. The expression of your soul. The life of Christ, His Spirit, the Divine Life or Source, allows you to be conscious at any moment. No matter who they are, every person has consciousness due to the Spirit of Christ. Apart from Him, nothing exists.

> *He himself is before all things and all things are held together in him.*
> Colossians 1:17 NET

This is where quantum physics (general revelation) and scripture (special revelation) come together. Scientists describe this field of energy based on accepted terminology. Scripture describes it differently, but it is the same thing. Everything was created and is held together by the Spirit of the Divine Life, the Source. And nothing exists apart from that Life.

Your consciousness and my consciousness are not separate. Neither is your consciousness and that of your friend or coworker. All consciousness is in Christ Jesus, the Divine Life. All things are in Christ, and Christ is in all things. If you are to live from within (from your spirit, the unseen), to the material (the seen), it is essential to understand this.

As you are one with Christ, so others are one with Christ. Thus, they are one with you. Quantum physics supports this. Look at the scriptures we quoted, and you will see the unseen field of energy in the Spirit of Christ.

Jesus and Paul could see things far off and be in places that were far off while still being physically in a different location. I Corinthians 2:16, as quoted earlier, makes it clear that we know Christ's mind because we have Christ's mind in the Spirit.

> *But he who is joined to the Lord is one spirit with Him.*
> 1 Corinthians 6:17 NKJV

There are not two spirits. There is one spirit together. His mind is your mind, and your mind is His. Everything you need at any moment lives within you, not outside you. Becoming aware of this and understanding its application to your life will change how you live.

Why go outside yourself when Christ's life and mind live within you?

In this unified field of energy, as everything is energy in Christ and held together each moment by Christ's life, you find your true self.

THE LIGHT SPECTRUM

Light is a fundamental concept of quantum physics and, thus, God's creation. It is described by the electromagnetic spectrum; a range of electromagnetic waves, forms of energy, that can travel through space. These waves vary in length, and each wavelength has unique properties and applications.

The electromagnetic spectrum increases in wavelength from right to left. On the left side of the spectrum, you have longer wavelengths (low frequency, low energy) like radio waves.

On the right side, you have shorter wavelengths (high frequency, high energy), like gamma rays. Let's go through the different parts of the spectrum and highlight this progression.

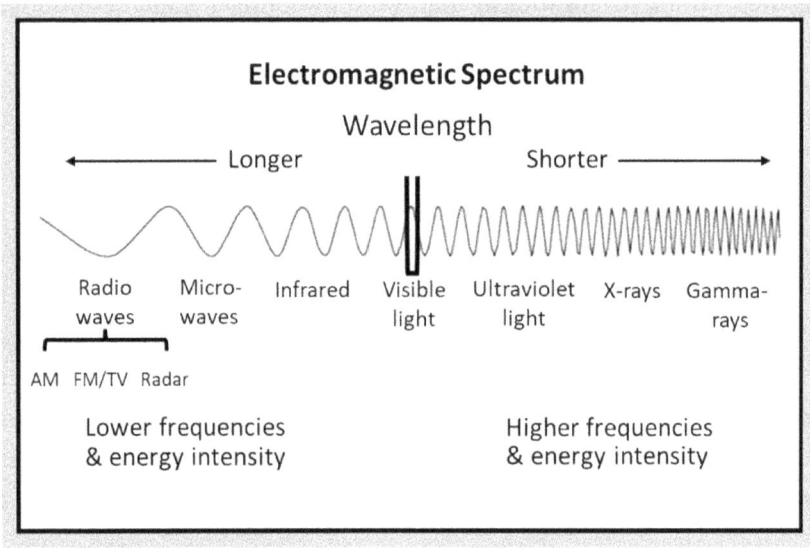

Figure 4.1 Electromagnetic Spectrum and the different wave patterns, frequencies, and energy intensities.

- **Gamma Rays**: Gamma rays have the shortest wavelengths in the electromagnetic spectrum. Nuclear reactions produce them and have high energy levels. Despite being harmful to living organisms, they have applications in cancer treatment and sterilization processes.
- **X-Rays**: Moving towards longer wavelengths, we encounter X-rays. While they are also high-energy waves, they have slightly longer wavelengths than gamma rays. X-rays are commonly

used in medical imaging to visualize bones and diagnose injuries or diseases.
- **Ultraviolet (UV) Waves**: UV waves have shorter wavelengths than visible light. They are responsible for sunburn and can cause damage to our skin. However, they also have important uses, such as sterilizing medical equipment and detecting counterfeit money.
- **Visible Light**: The visible light spectrum consists of different colors, each with its own wavelength. Starting from shorter wavelengths, we have violet, indigo, blue, green, yellow, orange, and red, in order of increasing wavelength. Visible light allows us to see the world around us and is responsible for the colors we perceive. Visible light makes up only 0.0035 percent of the electromagnetic spectrum. The human eye cannot see over 99 percent of all light waves.
- **Infrared Waves**: Infrared waves have longer wavelengths than visible light. We often feel them as heat. Infrared radiation is utilized in devices like remote controls and thermal imaging cameras, allowing us to control devices and see heat patterns.
- **Microwaves**: Microwaves have even longer wavelengths. They are used in microwave ovens for heating food quickly and evenly. Additionally, they play a crucial role in communication systems like satellite transmissions and wireless networks.
- **Radio Waves**: These waves have the longest wavelengths in the electromagnetic spectrum. They are used in various forms of communication, such as radio and television broadcasting, allowing us to listen to music, watch TV shows, and stay connected wirelessly.

As we discussed, visible light that our eyes can see makes up less than 1 percent of all light on the light spectrum. Of the light from our sun, 43 percent is visible, 52 percent is infrared, and 3 percent is ultraviolet.

The lower frequency radio and microwaves and the higher frequency X-rays and gamma rays make up the remaining 2 percent.

Unlike particles such as atoms, all light is made of photons, which do not have mass. These photons travel at 186,000 miles per second (speed of light). Light can travel 11,160,000 miles in one minute, and the light from our sun reaches the Earth in just over eight minutes. The distance from our planet to the next closest solar system in the Milky Way Galaxy is over 4.5 light-years away. We would need to travel at the speed of light to reach this solar system in 4.5 years. The fastest manned propulsion system that humanity has devised can travel around 35,000 miles per hour, requiring 84,000 years to travel the same distance. The universe God created is immense.

Jesus said, "I am the light of the world." Did He mean only visible light or all of the light on the electromagnetic spectrum? Did His listeners understand the various types and energy intensities of light? Did they understand frequencies and amplitudes in the light spectrum? He was making a general statement about what they knew and could understand, and He was metaphorically speaking of their soul and spirit, not light photons. Yet today, we have a greater understanding of this light spectrum than they had and have used these different wavelengths to communicate more effectively and even save lives. General revelation is continuous and will instruct us if we are open-minded and unafraid to receive it.

The Double-Slit Experiment and the Observer Effect

Light and atoms help us understand how the universe works. As we said earlier, light is made of energy called photons. Photons have no mass; they are just energy. Particles such as atoms have mass and are made of neutrons, protons, and electrons. Yet, when these photons and particles are measured or observed, they behave similarly. Their quirky behavior will give us insight into the general revelation of God's creation, the importance of where we place our attention and focus, and the power of our thoughts and emotions.

The double-slit experiment is a peek into the strange world of particles and light.[2] Imagine you have a wall with one slit in it, and you shoot little balls of light (photons) at it. They go through the slit and hit the other side, making a pattern resembling the slit's shape. So far, so good–it is as you would expect.

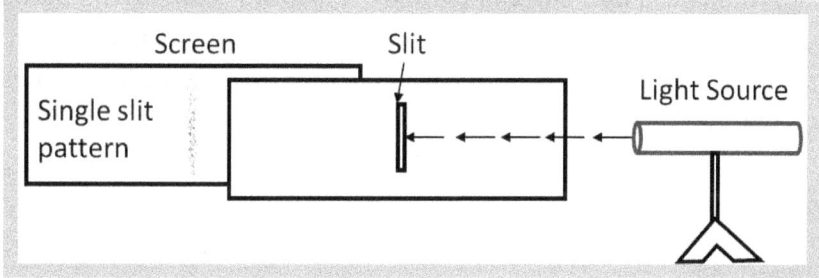

Figure 4.2 Double-slit experiment with one slit in the front wall with the screen behind it. The light pattern on the screen looks like a single slit, as would be expected.

Let us make things interesting by adding another slit next to the first one. If you shoot light through these two slits, something unusual happens. Instead of just making two patterns, the light starts acting like waves at the beach. It creates an interference pattern on the other side—bright and dark stripes, like ripples from water waves overlapping.

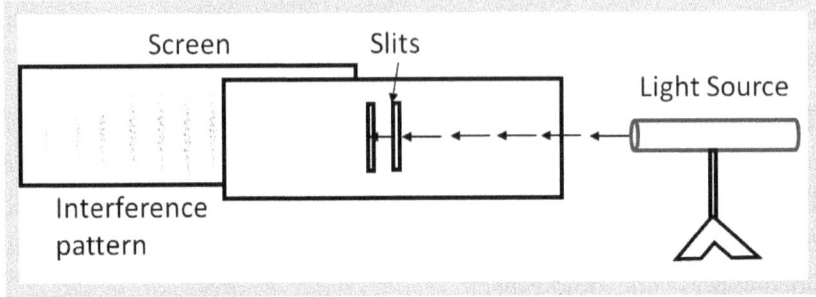

Figure 4.3 Double-slit experiment with two slits in the front wall with the screen behind it. Rather than making two patterns, they create an interference pattern with multiple lines on the back screen.

If you switch from light to electrons, very small particles like tiny marbles, and shoot them through the two slits individually, they should make two lines on the other side, like the slits. But they do not! Over time, these tiny particles also make a wave-like pattern, just like the light did.

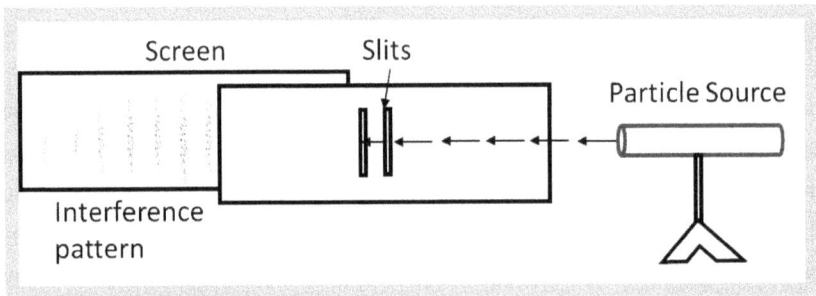

Figure 4.4 Double-slit experiment with two slits in the front with the screen behind it. When the tiny particles are shot through the slits, they create a wave-like interference pattern.

However, something strange happens when you try to watch which slit each particle goes through. The wave pattern disappears, and each particle acts as though it goes through just one slit. It is as if the particles somehow know they are being watched and change their behavior. The same is true for light photons when they are observed.

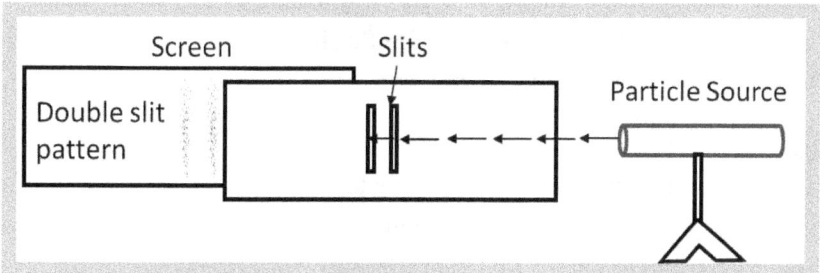

Figure 4.5 Double-slit experiment when the particles are being observed. The wave function that creates the interference pattern collapses, creating a particle pattern of the two slits.

This experiment shows that light which has no mass and particles with mass can behave like particles and waves. It is as if they are playing hide-and-seek with us, acting like particles when we watch them and showing their wave-like side when we are not looking.

This change in behavior due to observation highlights a fundamental aspect of the universe: measurement affects the behavior of light photons and particles. Observation collapses the wave-like behavior into a specific state. This phenomenon informs us of reality's nature, our observation's role, and the relationship between particles and waves.

Why would this be important for living a spiritual life? God's universe responds to our observation and attention. When we give attention and focus to anything, it impacts the outcome. We are co-creators with God

(I Corinthians 3:9), and this comes from the inner life of the Spirit, not through self-effort. We are seated with Christ in the heavenly places (Ephesians 2:6) and heirs to all that belongs to Christ (Romans 8:17), which is everything!

We manifest into the external world by focusing on our internal spiritual life. You go inward to live outwardly. That is the spiritual lesson of the double-slit experiment. The entire universe awaits your attention and focus so that in concert with the Spirit of Christ, who is one with your spirit, you may fulfill all you were created to experience and enjoy (Ephesians 2:10).

Light photons and the smallest subatomic particles respond to our observation. Amazing things can happen when we give our thoughts, intentions, and emotions to live in the reality of general revelation.

The Uncertainty Principle

The uncertainty principle is a fundamental concept in quantum physics that states there is a limit to how precisely we can know the position and momentum of a tiny particle, such as an electron. The more accurately we measure one property, the less accurately we can measure the other. This is not due to limitations in our tools but a fundamental characteristic of the quantum world.[3]

We love certainty—less stress, fewer surprises. But quantum physics flips that script: at its core, everything boils down to probabilities. The observer's choices can nudge outcomes, but no one can fully control exactly how or when something takes shape. Reality is not a neat chain of certainties; it is a field of possibilities unfolding beyond our complete command.

Jesus was walking with His disciples toward Jerusalem one day. He was hungry and came upon a fig tree, but it had no figs (Mark 11:12-14). He looked at the fig tree and said, "Let no one eat from you again," and He and the disciples went on their way. When they returned later that evening, the fig tree had withered and dried up from the roots. This surprised the disciples. But Jesus was practicing the realities of what the double-slit experiment proves and the uncertainty principle.

He spoke to the fig tree and commanded that no one eat from it again. He then went on His way. He did not try to control the outcome; He trusted it would occur. He did not try to determine when it would happen or how. He trusted that it would be the correct outcome whenever it occurred or how. He did not worry about people's thoughts if it did not happen immediately. He was not in the people-pleasing business. He gave His attention to the tree, spoke His word, and went on, trusting it would work out.

Jesus responded to the disciple's astonishment,

> *Have faith in God! I can guarantee this truth: This is what will be done for someone who doesn't doubt but believes what he says will happen: He can say to this mountain, 'Be uprooted and thrown into the sea,' and it will be done for him. That's why I tell you to have faith that you have already received whatever you pray for, and it will be yours.*
> Mark 11:22-24 GW

Faith is not asking and believing. Faith is seeing that the thing is done according to God and simply agreeing with gratitude and thanks (Hebrews 11:1). At the right time, it will manifest itself materially. Let go of the need for certainty of outcomes and trust the one who knows *your* best outcome.

Potential, Probability, and Possibility

Your chances of winning the lottery are about 1 in 302.6 million.[4] Even so, millions of people put down a few dollars every week just in case they guess the lucky combination of numbers. When living life in the Spirit, the odds are much more in your favor.

In the quantum realm, particles occupy multiple states at once; a phenomenon called superposition. But the instant we measure or observe them, all those potential outcomes collapse into a single reality; a process known as the observer effect. Imagine a spinning coin in a blurry mix of heads and tails while in the air. Only when you catch it and look at it does it settle into one side or the other. Similarly, in the quantum realm, particles seem to be in a combination of states until observed.

This observation-induced change can influence probabilities. Before observing, the chances of different outcomes are described by a mathematical concept called the wave function. The wave function collapses with your observation, and the particle takes on a definite state. This means that your act of observing affects the outcome and the probabilities of where the particle will be or what it will be doing.

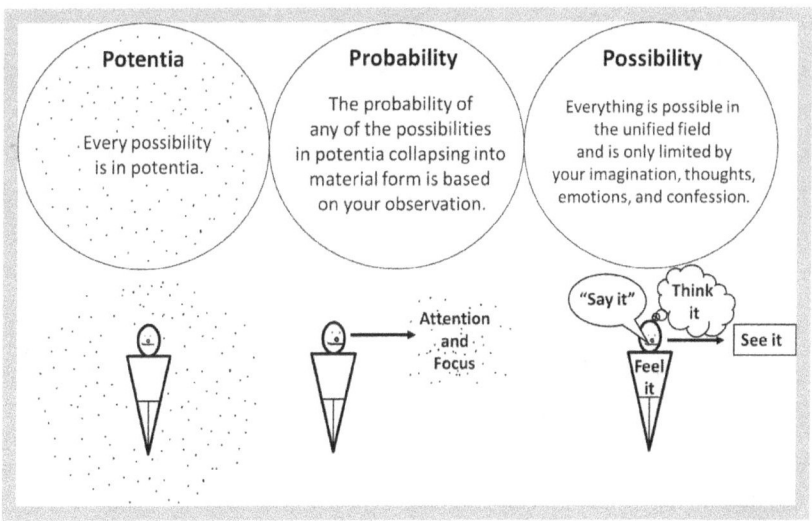

Figure 4.6 In quantum physics, every possible outcome is in potentia, or superposition. The probability of an outcome is based on your observation of the particles. The possibility of a particular outcome is only limited by your imagination, thoughts, emotions, and confession.

Figure 4.6 illustrates this phenomenon. Every possibility is in superposition. The Apostle Paul wrote,

> *Everything belongs to you. Whether it is Paul, Apollos, Cephas, the world, life, or death, present or future things, everything belongs to you. You belong to Christ, and Christ belongs to God.*
> I Corinthians 3:21-23 GW

Everything belongs to you. No matter what it is, every possibility is in superposition because all things are yours in Christ. The probability of it manifesting is based on your observation. Your attention, imagination, thoughts, emotions, and confession impact the outcome. Because all these things are part of giving your focus to something. God controls when, where, and how; you and I participate in the process each moment. We are co-heirs with Christ (Romans 8:17), so anything is possible. We are co-creators with Christ (I Corinthians 3:9), so it is our privilege to participate in everything.

The spiritual person is someone who lives from their inner life of spirit. In this inner life, everything is possible, and all the possibilities are in potentia or superposition. They are only limited by your willingness to participate. This participation is seeing what God sees, saying what God says about any matter, and then living in gratitude and thanks that it is so, even when it is not seen materially.

Spiritual people regularly manifest into this material world—not by self-effort, cleverness, worry, or greed for something they do not need, but by living each moment, in the moment, with their focus on their spirit in union with Christ's Spirit.

The book's second part will unpack how living from an inward spiritual reality works.

Part Two

How It Works

Chapter 5

Attention and the Power of Focus

You become what you give your attention to.

Epictetus

A research study was conducted to examine workers' average attention span using computers. This study was conducted over nineteen years, from 2004 to 2023. They did this by measuring how long an office worker spent on any task at the computer from the start of the task to when the worker chose to do something else, such as checking email or going to get coffee. In 2004, the average attention span was two and a half minutes. By 2012, that had declined to seventy-five seconds. By 2023, it was at forty-seven seconds. In nineteen years, the average attention span of an American office worker who uses a computer has gone from two and one-half minutes to forty-seven seconds.[1] That represents an attention span decline of 69 percent over this time period.

In a society that regularly checks their iPhones for email, text, internet, or the latest video app, our attention spans have decreased to less than that of many animals. Even the producers of sitcoms have come to understand this: The average scene can last less than ninety seconds.

Where Your Attention Goes, Your Energy Follows

Attention and focus are related cognitive processes, but they are distinct from each other in how they function. Attention is the ability to selectively concentrate on specific stimuli or information from the environment. It involves directing your mental resources to a particular thing or task while ignoring other distractions. Attention can be thought of as the gateway to perception. It determines what information enters your conscious awareness at any given moment. There are different types of attention, such as selective attention (focusing on one thing while ignoring others), divided attention (juggling between multiple tasks), and sustained attention (maintaining focus over an extended period, which we will discuss).

Focus refers to sustained and undivided attention on a single task or piece of information. It is the ability to maintain concentration on a specific target for an extended period. It is like zooming in on a single point and staying there. Focus often implies a deeper level of concentration, where you are fully immersed in a task or idea and can effectively block out other distractions.

In practical terms, having good attention skills helps you choose what to focus on. Being skilled at intense focus allows you to maintain attention on the selected target. Both attention and focus are vital for tasks that require deep thinking, learning, problem-solving, and overall cognitive performance.

Think of a photographer photographing a meadow next to a mountain range. The photographer would first pay attention to the mountain range and the meadow. She would then focus the camera on the meadow. Eventually, she would find an angle and specific spot she wanted to capture in her photo, but this would require focusing the camera until she had the shot she wanted.

Where we place our attention determines what we eventually focus on. What we focus on will ultimately determine the outcomes that manifest in our lives, similar to the photo the photographer would eventually capture as she focused the camera.

Where you place your attention is where your life energy flows. Jesus' life is an example of this.

> *Jesus said to the Jews, "I can guarantee this truth: The Son cannot do anything on his own. He can do only what he sees the Father doing. Indeed, the Son does exactly what the Father does."*
> John 5:19 GW

> *"But first, be concerned about his kingdom and what has his approval. Then all these things will be provided for you. So don't ever worry about tomorrow. After all, tomorrow will worry about itself. Each day has enough trouble of its own."*
> Matthew 6:33, 34 GW

To see what His Father was doing meant Jesus was focused on the Spirit, rather than external things. He listened in spirit and responded. He joined the Father in what He was doing and copied Him. This is life in the Spirit. Attention to our union in Christ captures our focus. Jesus said not to worry about tomorrow (not plan for tomorrow, which is different). Tomorrow will unfold as it is supposed to. It is not something you can control. Give your attention to the moment, focus on your life in Christ, the inward life in Him, and each moment is an opportunity to follow Him *in a way that is right for you*.[2]

Our energy flows to that which we give our attention and focus. We only have so much energy, so be judicious about your focus. Your outcomes depend on it.

Focus, Intention, and the Observer Effect

We have already discussed the observer effect. How does the observer effect and where we place our attention impact the outcomes in our lives? Observation affects the result when you focus on a specific outcome with a clear intention. For instance, when light was observed, it acted more like a particle than a wave. When light was unobserved, it acted like a wave. What made the change? The observation or measurement. Light responded to the measurement based on the intention of the one who measured it.

This has many applications, but none more significant than the reality that this world is interactive and responds to you based on where you place your attention and your intention. As we discuss in chapter two, Jesus taught us to set our attention and focus.

> *I can guarantee this truth: This is what will be done for someone who doesn't doubt but believes what he says will happen: He can say to this mountain, 'Be uprooted and thrown into the sea,' and it will be done for him. That's why I tell you to have* faith that you have already received whatever you pray for, *and it will be yours.*
> Mark 11:23-24 GW

Here is an example of focus with intention and the observer effect. "He can say to this mountain" was Jesus' way of emphasizing the impossibility of a situation, but that focus with clear intention can change it. He must focus first on the mountain to "Be uprooted and thrown into the sea." He intended all of the mountain to be cast into the sea. However, he must be willing to say it, then "it will be done for him." But not if he does not say it. That is the essence of faith: to see the thing that is already done, even when you cannot see it physically. To see it as completed and give your amen to it, "to have faith that you have already received whatever you pray for."

> *Faith assures us of things we expect and convinces us of the existence of things we cannot see.*
> Hebrews 11:1 GW

Faith is believing those things that are not as though they were because, with God, they are.[3] As we saw in chapter four, it already exists in potentia because every possible outcome already exists.

When we give our attention to something, with focus, our very observation of it impacts the outcome. But that outcome is based on an intention, which is faith—seeing it as already completed. Wishing and asking for it to be true has little or no impact. It must be something we are assured of, something of substance to us, though unseen. As real as any material thing we can see or touch.

Mindfulness: The Power of Focus

Meditation is described as mindfulness, the ability to focus on the now, this moment, while maintaining an inner calm and relaxed state.

> Meditation is a practice of mindfulness, or focusing the mind on a particular object, thought, or activity to train attention and awareness, and achieve a mentally clear and emotionally calm and stable state.[4]

There is no official definition of meditation or mindfulness. There are many ways to meditate, each with specific goals and benefits. What is important is that meditation is a tool for bringing your mind and body into the moment, capturing your attention, and focusing on a specific thing rather than on the past or the future.

Athletes use focus to train their bodies and minds to perform at a higher level than they could through physical talent alone. Students use focus to learn a body of material and then use that knowledge to pass a test. Pilots use focus to maintain a safe speed, altitude, and direction, eventually allowing the plane to land safely. Meditation allows one to unlock the power of focus and then use that focus in a positive way, similar to an athlete, student, or pilot.

Attention and focus are the beginning points of living from within. The key is training your attention to the moment and focusing on your spirit. Mindfulness allows you to be in the moment and block out the racing thoughts, negative emotions, and the to-do list that never stops calling you.

Mindfulness starts with focusing on your breath. Breathe in and count to five slowly, then slowly breathe out and count to five as you do. Breathe in again, counting to five, then slowly breathe out. Do this at least three to five times, focusing on your breath. When you focus on your breathing, you are focusing on your spirit. The word in Greek for spirit is *pneuma*, which means wind or breath, that which is unseen. As you focus on your breath, the body will slowly calm, and tension will recede. Now, you can bring your focus to your body.

As you focus on your body, you can start at your head. As you slowly breathe in and out, notice the area your head takes up in the space you occupy. Then, work your way down the neck, shoulders, hips, thighs, calves, ankles, and feet. Notice the space your body takes up in your room. Now, you are beginning to meditate, clearing your mind and focusing only on the moment.

This power of focus can be used anytime in any situation to bring you into the moment. The power of focus and your development of this skill will eventually determine your outcomes and whether you thrive or continue just to survive.

You Have the Life You Focus On

When clients come into my office, they tend to focus on the problems occurring in their lives. They see problems with bosses, relatives, spouses, children, friends, coworkers, career, money, health, and most importantly, their shortcomings and mistakes. They focus on people and things they have little or no control over. Yet, those things are simply symptoms of a more significant problem: where they have placed their focus. As one person has said, "The problem is your focus on the problem." We will never thrive inwardly or outwardly if we focus outwardly on material things or problems.

Taking responsibility is the first step to living from within. You have the life you focus on, which is your reality, and taking responsibility is necessary. This can be one of the more difficult things to accept. We tend to blame others for our situation. Maybe you believe it is your spouse and their attitude and actions that have hurt your marriage. Or your boss at work who never gives you an opportunity for a promotion. It could be the way your parents treated you growing up and their neglect or even abuse. We can even blame the government and those in authority for our problems. Christians are good at blaming the devil and his demons for harassing them and tempting them. I have heard this many times. Focusing on the devil and blaming him has taken priority over taking responsibility for choices. Blaming an unseen antagonist is much easier than looking at yourself in the mirror and being honest.

Your current life is due to where you have focused; either externally on problems, people, or things, or internally on the truth of your identity as one with the Divine Life. This includes seeing yourself as a spiritual being with a soul, experiencing a human life, and coming into the moment to bring your focus inward rather than outward. To realize you are more than your current circumstances, problems, or mistakes. You are a spiritual being, and there is nothing wrong with you. You are loved, valued, and accepted just as you are. God loves you as is. He would not change a thing. So, you can focus on loving yourself as you are, where you are, mistakes and failures included. This will do more than you can imagine. Be aware of who you are in each moment, loving that person, and you will begin to live from within, thrive in life, and fulfill your purpose for being here.

This world is an interactive one. Where you place your attention, and focus impacts the outcomes: remember the observer effect. The particles and light waves respond to your attention and focus; as we have seen, every possible outcome already exists in potentia. Your observation will impact the outcome. You are a co-creator, not a passive observer. You are actively involved in the results, whether you understand it or not. Jesus said, "He can say to this mountain, 'Be uprooted and thrown into the sea,' and it will be done for him." Are you ready to move mountains? In the next chapter, we will look at how that works.

Chapter 6

Intention, Imagination, and Vision

Imagination is the voice of daring. If there is anything Godlike about God it is that. He dared to imagine everything.[1]

Henry Miller

Throughout history, the human capacity for imagination and invention has been a driving force behind transformative breakthroughs. Visionary thinkers have conceptualized ideas that, despite initial skepticism or challenges, shaped the course of history and propelled society into new frontiers. Three remarkable stories stand out as a testament to the power of visionary thinking and imagination, each highlighting the extraordinary vision of individuals who dared to imagine possibilities beyond the constraints of their time.

In the late 15th century, Leonardo da Vinci, a true Renaissance genius, envisioned and sketched a flying machine that anticipated the principles of modern aviation. His ornithopter design aimed to replicate the motion of bird wings, with flapping wings attached to a central frame.

Although da Vinci never built a functional prototype, his detailed sketches and understanding of aerodynamics laid the groundwork for future aviation pioneers. His imaginative exploration of flight influenced the evolution of aircraft design.²

In 1877, Thomas Edison introduced the world to the phonograph, marking a transformative moment in the history of sound recording. Edison's inventive mind led him to imagine a device capable of recording and reproducing sound. The phonograph featured a rotating cylinder covered in a grooved surface, capturing sound vibrations through a stylus. His ground-breaking invention revolutionized the music and entertainment industry, providing a means to preserve and share audio recordings. The phonograph laid the foundation for subsequent developments in audio technology, leading to the creation of modern recording devices.³

In 1989, a British computer scientist, Tim Berners-Lee, proposed an innovative concept that would reshape how humanity interacts with information—the World Wide Web (WWW). Berners-Lee envisioned a decentralized system where documents linked through hyperlinks could be accessed and shared globally. With the creation of the first web browser and server, he implemented this vision, giving birth to the internet as we know it today. The WWW transformed communication, information dissemination, and business practices, becoming integral to daily life. His imaginative idea connected people across the globe and laid the foundation for the digital age and the rapid evolution of technology.⁴

These stories exemplify the extraordinary capacity of human imagination and invention, demonstrating how visionary thinkers have shaped history and propelled society into new frontiers through their creative ideas and innovations. The same is true for you and me. The Spirit allows us to use our imagination through a sharp vision led by purposeful intention. We are co-creators with the Source of all life each moment. The same creativity that lives in Christ lives in you.

And it is the natural course of each person who lives from their spirit.

Purposeful Intention

Intention and purpose are closely related concepts, yet they have distinct meanings. Intention refers to an individual's immediate, conscious aim or plan behind a specific action. It is the deliberate choice or plan to do something, often driven by personal desires, goals, or motives. Intention is focused on the present moment and the conscious decision-making process.

Purpose extends beyond immediate actions and involves a broader, long-term perspective. Purpose is the reason something exists or is done, providing a sense of direction and meaning to one's life or endeavors. It encompasses the overarching goals and objectives that guide actions over an extended period, contributing to a more profound sense of fulfillment and significance.

Intention is the deliberate choice made in the present, while purpose involves a broader, enduring reason that gives meaning to ongoing actions and decisions. Both play crucial roles in shaping individual experiences and directing personal growth.

Imagine a person deciding to build a new home. They might be motivated by the desire for more space, a better layout, or simply a place that feels more aligned with their lifestyle. In this case, the conscious intention is the active decision to start construction—driven by the immediate rewards of comfort, aesthetics, or improved daily living.

But the deeper purpose behind building this home could be far more meaningful. Perhaps it is about creating a sanctuary for loved ones, establishing long-term stability, or crafting a legacy to pass down. The true purpose stretches beyond bricks and blueprints—it is about shaping a foundation for years of memories, growth, and peace of mind. This enduring purpose continues to influence decisions long after the final nail is hammered. As you begin to live in the moment, it is important to do so with purposeful intention based on spiritual insight and truth. Living in the moment is directly tied to purposeful intention.

Imagination Brings Intention to Life

Disney's Imagineering program, formally known as Walt Disney Imagineering (WDI), is the creative force behind the conceptualization, design, and construction of Disney theme parks, attractions, resorts, and cruise ships worldwide.

Imagineering's hallmark is its innovative approach to storytelling through immersive experiences. This involves creating detailed environments that transport guests to different worlds, whether it is the futuristic landscapes of Tomorrowland, the whimsical realms of Fantasyland, or the adventurous spirit of Adventureland. This process is crucial to integrating cutting-edge technology with traditional artistic methods. Imagineers use advanced robotics, animatronics, digital media, and special effects to enhance the guest experience, ensuring each attraction is entertaining and technologically impressive.

Imagineering begins with blue sky brainstorming sessions, *where no idea is too outrageous*. This phase encourages creativity and exploration of all possibilities. Once a concept is selected, the project moves into design and development, where storyboards, scale models, and prototypes are created. The final phase involves construction and installation, meticulously crafting every detail to maintain Disney's lofty standards of quality and immersion.

Over the years, Imagineering has been responsible for iconic attractions such as Pirates of the Caribbean, The Haunted Mansion, and the various iterations of Space Mountain. Imagineering's influence extends beyond the parks to Disney's resorts and cruise lines, where thematic design and storytelling remain key elements.

Anyone can use their imagination if they are willing. You have the innate ability to be creative and imagine things as though they were already so. While some people have practiced using their imagination more than others, and some may have a greater predisposition to the creative side, everyone can practice and use the tool of imagination to their benefit.

Left-brain and right-brain thinking suggest that each brain hemisphere controls distinct types of thinking and behavior. This theory originated from the research of Roger W. Sperry, a Nobel Prize-winning neuropsychologist. The brain's left hemisphere is often associated with logical, analytical, and detail-oriented thinking. It is considered responsible for:

- **Language**: Processing words, syntax, and grammar.
- **Mathematics**: Handling numbers and logical reasoning.
- **Critical Thinking**: Analyzing information and making reasoned judgments.
- **Sequential Processing**: Understanding and organizing information linearly and orderly.

The brain's right hemisphere is linked to more holistic, intuitive, and creative thinking. It is thought to handle:

- **Creativity**: Art, music, and spatial abilities.
- **Emotional Processing**: Recognizing and expressing emotions.
- **Holistic Thinking**: Seeing the big picture and patterns.
- **Imagination**: Daydreaming and visualization.

While modern neuroscience suggests that the brain is more integrated than this dichotomy implies, it is helpful to understand that we all can use the tool of imagination. Using your imagination brings your intention to life.

Continuing with the house illustration, once you have written out your intention it is time to imagine yourself in the home. Here are tips to help you begin to imagine it as already completed:

- While meditating, take the written notes regarding your intention and begin to see it as colorfully as possible. What are the colors? What does it smell like? How does it feel to be in the house?
- Now, imagine yourself approaching the house and opening the door. Imagine yourself in the kitchen cooking or enjoying time with family or friends.
- See yourself walking into every room like an outside observer, just watching yourself. See it in as much detail as possible. Imagine your spouse or significant other living with you and enjoying the home. Imagine walking outside the house onto the patio enjoying coffee or wine. What does it feel like? Is there a breeze? Is it warm or cold? All of this is vitally important.
- Finally, allow yourself to imagine outside the box. Nothing is impossible. What would it look like if you could imagine something way outside the box? Nothing is good or bad; it is just your intention, purpose, and creative imagination working with the Source of all life. As Jesus said, *"all things are possible with God"* (Mark 10:27). And remember, the Source of all life, the universe if you will, does not respond to what you want; it responds to who you are this moment (Hebrews 11:1, *faith is substance and evidence,* both are present tense).

Visualizing a Completed Work

Once you have set your intention and spent some time imagining the possibilities, it is time to visualize what you have imagined as completed. *The universe does not respond to what you want. It responds to who you are.* The manifestation of anything requires vision. Until you see it as completed, in detail, it remains a possibility (as we saw in the double-slit experiment). The more you see it as completed in your mind's eye or vision, the more it becomes who you are. The energy vibration you resonate with is what the universe will respond to.

For instance, if you want to have a particular job, can you visualize the job? What would you do there? What is your title? How much money would you make? Can you close your eyes and see the office and the place where it is located? Can you see yourself driving to work, parking, and going inside? You need to see it with as much detail and clarity as possible. This is a skill you develop to participate with your spirit. Learn to go to your spirit to visualize the possibilities. Let your spirit give you the vision, and then work with the spirit to refine it.

Every tall commercial office building must first be a vision in someone's mind before it can manifest in a physical structure. Someone must have a vision of where it would be located and what the building would look like outside and inside. They need to have a vision of what materials would be used to construct it, what kind of tenants would be in the building, and how many stories it would eventually have. Only then can they take their dream to an architect to begin the process of sketching the structure and planning the details. But the key to all this is opening your mind to the possibilities.

Closed-minded people accomplish little and create barriers for others who have a vision. However, this is part of the process of capturing a vision and helping others see it. Overcoming opposition is part of the journey to a fully functioning vision.

Spirit can give you vision. Ego will lead you to respond in fear, desire control, and seek advantage over others. Spirit will bring you inward to your higher self and a vision that reflects who you are in spirit and soul. The higher self will give you a vision that serves others and fulfills your true purpose for this life.

Seeing something before it is reality, in your mind's eye, requires practice. It is a learned skill that all of us can do. I encourage you to practice developing a vision in everything you undertake. Consider these helpful tips:

- Meditate each day, practicing mindfulness and being in the moment. Take five to ten minutes in the morning and before bedtime. See chapter twelve for more on meditation. Focus on what you specifically want to visualize. Focus, focus, focus. That is the key.
- Anything is possible if you can see it and visualize it. But you must first believe it is possible (imagination) before you can visualize it. Jesus made this clear in His life and teachings (Mark 11:22-24).

See It as Completed

The goal is to see your vision completed and imagine yourself enjoying it now. The more you see it completed, the easier it is to feel gratitude and thankfulness. Can you see it as a completed work? Can you see yourself in it? Can you live in the present moment of that vision based on your purposeful intention?

Let us return to the illustration of the commercial building. Think of any commercial building near you (or you can use the house illustration instead). It could be a retail establishment, hotel, office building or industrial building. Now, stop and look at the land on which the building is located. It might have been an empty field or grove of trees before it was built. Someone had to use their skill of purposeful intention and visualization to see the building on that plot of land. The vision would not come to life if they had only seen the field or trees. They had to see it completed. They needed to walk into the building and enjoy its spaciousness and beauty as if it were already there. Then, they needed

Intention, Imagination, and Vision

to visualize themselves and others enjoying the building in as much detail as possible, as if the building had been built and completed and people were using it. It is essential that you see the vision and yourself in it as though it is already done—present tense, not future tense.

- "I have _____," NOT "I want _____," or "I wish I had _____."
- "I *have* _____," NOT "I will have _____," that doesn't work.

Use the left brain to develop purposeful intention, then use the right side to imagine and visualize what it looks like and how it would look with you specifically. Then, use both the left and right sides of your brain to bring it into the present moment. "I have the house I want at this moment." "I have the beige brick house I want this moment." "I have the beige brick house and enjoy coffee on the back porch now." Let them work together to develop, visualize, imagine, and bring into the present moment what you desire.

A Brief Word About Ego

Your true ego represents your specific behavioral style, talents, intellect, and emotional makeup. It is essential to love your true ego: how you are wired and how you work. Loving yourself, the true you, protects you from your false ego and allows you to love others for who they are in the Source of all life.

The false ego, or flesh, represents your attempts to deal with trauma, hurt, and disappointments through outward things rather than the inner reality of your value and worth in oneness with the Source of all life. Without this healing, you will seek things outwardly to compensate for how you feel about yourself inwardly. You will also maintain control to avoid pain and disappointment.

Thus, instead of seeking a home for its benefits to you and others, you will want a house to build up your wounded self-identity, to fit in with a particular group, or because it is a status symbol. None of these things are reasons to own a home. Your identity is the Source of all life and always has been. A new home will not change that or make you complete. A new home could damage your finances if you cannot make the payments. The Apostle Paul put it this way,

> *But I say, live by the Spirit and you will not carry out the desires of the flesh.*
> Galatians 5:16 NET

Let me bring this forward two thousand years into a modern understanding of this verse: *"It is my observation that if you live by your inner spirit-soul, the true you, then you will not fall prey to the attempts of your wounded unhealed inner ego to try and feel better about yourself."* As a spiritual coach, I have found that people fall into this trap often because they have not done the inner work of healing needed to operate freely of the false ego and its dictates.

I encourage you to read my first book, *Alignment of Authentic Love: Living Your Highest Life,* if you have not done the inner work required to heal and enjoy your life. Otherwise, you can fall prey to the desires of the false ego to get something externally to feel better about yourself internally. The only thing that truly helps is going inwardly to your spirit-soul and receiving the healing you need there.

The next chapter will examine how this manifesting process requires high-energy vibrations of gratitude, joy, and thankfulness. And how it is possible to always live in a state of gratitude so you can consistently manifest in your life.

Chapter 7

The High Energy of Gratitude

Gratitude to gratitude always gives birth.

Sophocles

Thanksgiving, instituted by Congress in the 1800s, is a federal holiday in the United States. It is celebrated on the third Thursday of November each year. We thank God for our shared and individual prosperity and blessings on this day.

This sense of gratitude is a fundamental part of the holiday as a nation. To be genuinely grateful and to express that gratitude.

Research on gratitude's impact reveals significant benefits for mental and physical health. People who practice gratitude experience reduced stress levels, enhanced emotional resilience, and improved mental health.[1] Studies have demonstrated that gratitude can lower cortisol, the stress hormone, resulting in better cardiac function and greater emotional stability. It is a high-energy emotion that influences and promotes physical health, productive relationships, and mental well-being.[2]

When you resonate with grateful vibrations, the universe's natural order attracts that energy to you. If you are filled with feelings of gratitude, you will attract grateful people. The same is true if you are thankful, you will attract thankful people. And if you are filled with joy, you will attract joyful people. The higher the feeling of gratitude, the greater the vibration and frequency. It is this high vibration (intensity) and frequency (high or low) that helps us to live from within and manifest outwardly into the material world.

Emotions and Thoughts Are Energy and Frequency

Based on scientific research, science has shown that emotions and thoughts are generated by complex biochemical and neurological activity in the brain and body.[3] These biochemicals and neurons are made of energy, so by their very nature, emotions and thoughts are part of that energy.

The double-slit experiment clarifies that where we place our attention and then focus impacts the outcome. Because they are energy, these emotions and thoughts affect the quantum field and attract like energy, thus helping to collapse the wave function into material form. In other words, the observer's emotional state and mental focus impact the outcome.

When someone enters my office, I immediately notice their emotional state (vibration and frequency). I am an empath, so this is normal for me. Those with lower vibrations and frequency usually express an emotional state of ingratitude, anger, bitterness, resentment, and self-hatred. I am not criticizing this. That is why they are in my office. I can even sense these low vibrations when I counsel over long distances through online video. Their beliefs about God, themselves, and others align with the lower vibrations and frequencies they give off. They will often confess these self-defeating and negative beliefs in our sessions that match the emotional state in which they are vibrating. Usually, they are unaware that they are confessing these things as they speak with me.

Have you ever had someone walk into a meeting with a high positive vibe and energy? Merely their presence in the room raised the mood of others in the meeting and created an atmosphere more conducive to productivity. This is evidence that emotions and thoughts epitomize energy and frequency.

I had a friend who was a high school cheerleader. She was vivacious, outgoing, and had a high vibe. I enjoyed being around her and the energy she gave off. She loved who she was, which showed in her relationships and participation as a cheerleader. No matter how bad the score was, she was unwavering with a positive vibe and high energy. Cheering on others can raise the emotional energy and the positive feelings of a large group of people.

That does not mean we all have to go around with high energy and always feel gratitude. Sometimes, we are tired, depressed, and sad, vibrating at a lower energy and frequency. It is part of being human. However, what matters is the awareness of how you feel and your willingness to generate feelings of gratitude when you are focused on a vision and imagining yourself in what you desire. In time, these higher vibrations of gratitude and thankfulness will attract the people, things, and opportunities you are focused on.

What We Think and Feel Is What We Attract

Our false ego, the self, desires to maintain control. It is driven by a desire to avoid pain due to unresolved traumas, hurts, and disappointments. This false ego focuses on everything other than higher emotional vibrations of gratitude, thanksgiving, and joy. Instead, it focuses on old destructive thoughts and the feelings tied to them from the memory banks of our brains. In time, the energy vibrations matching those negative thoughts and energy attract like energy. For instance, if you wake up each morning and repeat low-vibrational and low-frequency negative self-talk, such as:

- I am a hopeless case.
- I am worthless.
- I am not lovable.
- I will always be poor.
- I will never find someone to marry.
- Something bad always happens to me.

Then, people and experiences that resonate with your emotional frequency will be attracted to your life.

I had a client who believed everything she did and every relationship she had would eventually fall apart. No matter what she did, she thought it would not work out. She was constantly down on herself and felt hopeless, inadequate, and worthless. Unsurprisingly, she attracted people who would affirm these thoughts and feelings into her life. That was the level at which they vibrated in their emotions and thoughts. It was a vicious cycle that was destructive and frustrating to her. In time, we worked to raise her vibrations of gratitude and increase her self-awareness. She began to see herself as worthy of love, acceptance, and success in her endeavors. This change in her inner emotions and beliefs helped her improve her financial condition and choose healthy friendships that encouraged and built her up. It even allowed her to change the church she attended to one that encouraged her in the love of a good God.

I had the opportunity to do executive coaching with a woman who was the senior vice president of a financial firm. She was struggling to make decisions on an important project that would impact the direction of the company's products and services. When we first talked, it became clear that she struggled with self-doubt and fear of failure. As we "peeled the onion," she revealed feelings of insecurity, inadequacy, and hopelessness. Much of this had to do with how she saw herself from unresolved hurts in her relationship with her dad. He was a very demanding person who never complimented or encouraged her in any way. She could not escape the memories of his criticism and exacting standards. We began by exploring how she saw herself and her decision-making process. We then worked on increasing self-awareness and identifying how she felt and why. This freed her to focus on the project's goals, visualize what she wanted, and imagine it as already done. Her energy levels increased, and she felt grateful for it. After significant work, she completed the project, built consensus and agreement across multiple departments, and created a new direction for the products the company offered its clients.

Imagine waking up every day with a high-energy vibration of gratitude and thankfulness. Instead of the negative self-defeating low-vibration self-talk, you could reverse it by feeling and saying,

- I am *confident* and *assured* of my abilities and strengths.
- I am of *great value* and *worth*.
- I am *lovable*.
- I am *wealthy*, and money comes to me every day.
- I *have* friends who encourage and support me.
- It is incredible how good things *always happen* to me.

Imagine how this would help raise your emotional vibrations and frequency and attract what you visualize, imagine, and desire.

Gratitude Is the Emotion of Faith

Faith is not trying to believe, hoping you receive. Faith is seeing that you have received it and acting like you already have it.

Faith believes those things that are not, as though they were because, with God, they are.
Manley Beasley

Now faith is the substance of things hoped for, the evidence of things not seen.
Hebrews 11:1 NKJV

Faith is the substance and evidence that you have it. If you believe you already have something, gratitude is a natural emotion. It is the emotion of faith. Faith sees it as done and is naturally grateful.

Gratitude springs from the substance and evidence of faith, which sees it as completed. Faith brings it from the future into the present. We have been told that believing is seeing. The Apostle Paul wrote,

For we walk by faith and not by sight.
II Corinthians 5:7 NKJV

But this is a misunderstanding of the passage. The word walk has the idea of conducting one's life. Faith is how we conduct our life. But whose faith? The faithfulness of Jesus. We see the finished work of God in Christ and His faithfulness. Sight is from the Greek root word *eidos*, which primarily speaks of seeing things from an outward physical form. Therefore, "not by sight" indicates that faith should lead us to an inner knowing or seeing. Seeing inwardly that something is already done and completed allows us to feel gratitude and eventually give thanks that we have it. It is now brought into the present moment.

This is what the universe responds to, not what we want, but what we see inwardly through the eyes of faith and then feel through the high energy of gratitude.

When I started this ministry in 2017, I had a vision. I wanted to teach what I was learning and counsel people on how to thrive and enjoy life, not just survive it. I was not thinking about money; I was grateful I had whatever I needed. Several months later, a friend called me and wanted to meet at my home. When he arrived, he explained how he felt led to give to the ministry I had started. He handed me a check to sustain the ministry for several years. I was astonished. After he left, I realized something: money comes to those with vision and imagination who see it as already done.

To start the ministry, I created a nonprofit organization in the U.S. and named it Abiding in Agape. Then I acted as though I already had everything I needed for it, and the universe, built to respond to my present-tense feelings and actions, responded with a check.

Gratitude is the emotion of faith, and faith is seeing the unseen, which is already complete. Would you be willing to see inwardly what is already completed in the faithfulness of Christ and, with gratitude, raise your vibrations to match it?

Thankfulness Is the Result of Gratitude

In the early days of the ministry, I conducted spiritual coaching for free. I encouraged people to give what they could but did not require them to do so. Over the years, I have learned much from those who chose to give and those who gave little or nothing. Those who have given freely and generously to the ministry's support live in tremendous gratitude and, thus, thankfulness. Their energy is one of gratitude, giving, and receiving because you cannot give without receiving (Luke 6:38; Acts 20:35). They also make the most significant strides in recovering from past trauma, hurt, and disappointments. Their relationships tend to improve more rapidly, and their finances become healthier. When someone lives in gratitude, in the moment, it is natural for them to feel thankful, which leads to giving back. Gratitude leads to thankfulness, which is the natural next step. Thankfulness in the heart leads to living in more intense vibrations and higher frequencies. These higher vibrations and frequencies of thankfulness result in you actively living in the present. One who is thankful must, by necessity, live in the moment. You can be thankful for something in the past, but to express that thankfulness, you must feel it and be willing to acknowledge it.

In other words, what you put into something is what you will eventually get out of it. If thankfulness is what you express, then the actions of thankfulness will follow. Those feelings and actions will benefit others, increasing your vibrations and frequency. It is a circle that continues upwards.

When I became ill with a neurological condition that created great pain in my extremities, foggy brain, fatigue, and loss of weight, I faced a challenge. Would I sulk in self-pity, feeling sorry for myself in a pool of negativity and bitterness, or find a way to function the best I could? I suffered from depression and discouragement due to the illness and its effects. I was challenged to change my focus and thinking.

> *In everything give thanks; for this is the will of God for you in Christ Jesus.*
> I Thessalonians 5:18 NASB

Could I give thanks for this illness and the benefits that would accrue to me, even though I could not see them now? Each morning, I began to feel grateful that I could walk, feel my feet, and care for myself. I would give thanks for the day, the opportunities it afforded, and the moment. Each moment was a gift, and I felt grateful to have had that moment. I found my nerve pain, foggy brain, and fatigue subsiding. I stopped losing weight, and my overall mental health began to improve. In time, I began to see God as a God of love and kindness, not one of anger, retribution, and punishment. I began to reconstruct my theology around these facts and began to feel better internally and function more effectively externally. But the impetus for all of this was gratitude and thankfulness.

The universe responds to who you are, not what you want. What are you giving the universe to respond to? You can create your feelings. Did you know that? You can. It is a fact.[4] That does not mean every feeling can be controlled, but the feelings of gratitude and thankfulness can be generated internally when you choose to do so. I am a living example of that. It may seem a little weird at first, but as you focus inward on your spirit, one with the Source of all life, you discover that the Source is Love. And when we love, He fills us with gratitude and thankfulness. That gratitude and thankfulness lives in you right now; accept it is there to access and enjoy it. How we do that is the focus of the next chapter.

Chapter 8

The Power of Thoughts and Words

If you want to change your life, you have to change your thoughts and your words. Out of this will flow changes that you can hardly imagine.

Louise Hay

The placebo effect is a well-documented phenomenon in which patients experience real improvements in their health condition after receiving treatment with no therapeutic benefit. This improvement is driven by the patient's belief in the treatment's effectiveness. The power of the mind in influencing physical health is evident in numerous studies where placebos—such as sugar pills or saline injections—have led to measurable health benefits.[1]

The doctor's words are not just words; they are potent tools that can shape a patient's expectations and belief in a treatment. When a doctor communicates with confidence and reassurance, it can significantly enhance a patient's positive expectations, leading to a stronger placebo effect. This understanding can enlighten us about the power of words in influencing our beliefs and, consequently, our experiences.[2]

The role of the patient's thoughts is just as important. If the patient believes the medication is of therapeutic value, can help with the physiological condition, and should be taken, then the placebo effect is enhanced.

This verbal communication sets the stage for the mind-body interaction that underpins the placebo effect. Positive expectations can trigger the brain to release endorphins and other neurochemicals that mimic the effects of actual treatments. Belief in the treatment can lead to physiological changes, such as reduced pain, improved mood, and enhanced overall well-being. This illustrates the profound connection between mental and physical health, emphasizing that the mind's perception can alter bodily functions.

In this chapter, we will see how our thoughts ultimately lead to what we confess and say to ourselves. These thoughts and confessions, negative or positive, attract and impact what manifests in our lives. The field of energy that everything is connected to operates based on our observation, what we focus on, what we imagine, feel, and eventually confess. Just as the placebo confession leads to healing in the patient, the confession of each individual leads to a particular outcome. *Remember, the universe responds to what you are, not what you want.*

Thoughts Lead to Confessions

Hunter came to see me because he had problems maintaining relationships, career challenges, and stable finances. As we looked at past traumas, hurts, and disappointments, he began to see how his father's actions had impacted him. His father was a critical person who would call his children derogatory names, telling them they were worthless, always a disappointment to him, and incapable of doing anything. Every weekend, his father would get drunk at the bar down the street and come home and beat him, his brother, and their mother. He was so afraid of his father's outbursts that he would hide under the bed and fall asleep there, hoping his father would not find him when he came home from the bar.

He felt insecure, worthless, inadequate, hopeless, and rejected. His self-identity was: "Something is wrong with me; I am just a failure; I am unlovable." These identities caused him to sabotage relationships with women once they became serious for fear the women would eventually reject him. It was better for him to break off the relationship than for them to reject him and break it off.

He would sabotage his career by turning down opportunities for job promotions and procrastinating on his work due to fear of failure and rejection. His finances were unstable because he spent most of his money on cars, trips, and sporting events. His credit card debt was well over what he earned in a year, and he sometimes struggled to make his house payment.

He would constantly tell himself, "You're just a loser; you can't do anything right; you're so worthless; no one could love you." And these were just a few of the things he thought and confessed about himself.

Having identified these wounded emotions and false identities in our sessions, he began to work on letting go of the wounded emotions and reprogramming his mind with the truth of his worth and value. He would use a feelings worksheet to identify how he felt each day, and I AM affirmations to help in that process. He would look in the mirror and speak the truth of his value and worth in God's eyes rather than repeating what his father had told him for years. We would also work on these affirmations together in our sessions.

In time, he began to confess the reality of his value and worth and to heal from the emotional wounds of the past. He even learned to forgive those who had harmed him, such as his father. *But primarily, he started to love himself, his true self, who was of great worth and value. Without loving yourself as you are, for who you are, it is impossible to love others who are created in God's image and likeness, which is key to thriving in this earthly existence.*

In time, he started dating a woman and reached the sixth-month mark with her; a record for him. He also began a new position with a company doing something he loved and was good at, which helped reduce his procrastination and avoiding greater responsibility issues. Eventually, his finances became stable as he proactively worked to live within a budget. Above all, he was thinking differently and confessing the truth he now believed. He began to think and say loving things about himself; the essence of who he was, which is spirit-soul.

What you think and say has incredible power. No amount of physical effort can overcome negative thoughts and verbal confessions a person makes. Ultimately, the universe will bring you what you think and say about yourself. It can be no other way. You really are creating your world by what you say and confess in the quantum field of energy that the Source of all life created.

Awareness of Thoughts and Words

When coaching business leaders, I always want to know their level of self-awareness. Are they aware of their thoughts, feelings, and actions and how they impact their job and those they work with? If they lack self-awareness, which is usually the case, then this is the area we focus on first. Because thoughts and words create the world you have, it is essential to develop the skill of self-awareness. And make no mistake, it is a skill developed through practice.

The most effective way to develop self-awareness is mindfulness, which can be practiced daily through meditation. With meditation, thoughts are focused on the moment, not past mistakes or fears of the future.

Meditation helps self-awareness in many important ways:

- **Stress Reduction**: Meditation is widely recognized for reducing stress. Techniques like mindfulness meditation can help lower cortisol levels, the stress hormone, which can reduce symptoms of stress-related disorders.[3]
- **Enhanced Concentration**: Regular meditation can improve concentration and focus. Mindfulness exercises can increase mental clarity and attention span.[4]
- **Anxiety Management**: Meditation can lead to reductions in anxiety levels. Mindfulness and other meditation techniques can help manage and even reduce the symptoms of anxiety disorders.[5]
- **Improved Emotional Health**: Some forms of meditation can improve self-image and give people a more positive outlook on life. Mindful meditation, for example, can help enhance self-awareness and reduce symptoms of depression.[6]
- **Mindfulness in Daily Activities**: Regular meditation can help you remain present and engaged in daily activities, reducing the tendency to react automatically or unconsciously.[7]

Reducing stress allows you to be in the moment and aware of what you are thinking and saying. Many people are unaware of what they say or how they say it. Clients who feel stressed out have told me, "Everything I do turns into a mess." They continue speaking, oblivious to what they just said or the power that every thought and statement carries. With that negative thought and confession alone, they have done more to determine the future outcome of an endeavor than any amount of effort or work they could produce.

Enhancing concentration allows for greater internal awareness, which assists in being aware of what you are thinking and saying. Meditation, by its very nature, assists in concentrating on the moment. That concentration trains the brain to be more aware of what you say and do. Our brain is often not trained to be aware of thoughts and words.

Thus, we repeat negative things, sometimes over and over, like a mantra, poisoning our lives and desires.

Anxiety can overwhelm us like a tsunami, causing us to lose sight of reality in any situation. In this state, people do things they might not normally do, such as thinking and saying things that hurt their well-being and desires for the future. Meditation can act as a guard against the ups and downs of anxiety. Meditation allows you to focus on your breathing and your body. By doing so, you slow your breathing, calming your body down.

Focusing on a positive self-image while meditating will naturally improve how you feel about yourself. If you begin to love yourself, it is much less likely that your thoughts and words will be ones of self-loathing and deprecation. Instead, your thoughts and words will be positive and self-affirming, which impacts how the universe responds to you.

Most of my clients struggle with low self-esteem due to the traumas, hurts, and disappointments of the past. As they focus on I AM affirmations, they begin to see they are worthy of love and respect. In time, they can release negative self-thoughts and replace them with the truth of their union in the Divine Life. From this comes words of self-love and care, which the quantum field of energy then responds to.

The greatest gift you can give yourself is greater self-awareness, especially of thoughts, words, actions, and feelings. Jesus said it this way,

> *I tell you, you can pray for anything, and if you believe that you've received it, it will be yours.*
> Mark 11:24 NLT

Jesus emphasizes, "Believe that you've received it." Present tense! Can you see that it is already yours at this moment? That is why awareness of what you think and say is so important. "I have it, thank you" leads you to the fulfillment of that thing. "I will never have it" leads you to more of the same failure and frustration. Awareness helps us, by the spirit, to strategically direct our thoughts and words.

Homologeo: Agreeing with the Source

Homologeo is a Greek compound word from *homos*, meaning "the same," and *lego*, to "speak to a conclusion." Thus, complete agreement or common confession. It is agreeing and saying the same thing about any given thing or situation.

The biggest problems are not your current circumstances, husband, wife, family, friends, coworkers, career, finances, health, material possessions, or the wrongs others have committed against you. None of that is the real issue. The main issue is your unwillingness to confess in agreement with the Source of all life that what He says is true about you in union with Him. That is the problem.

There will be little to no progress until there is a common confession between you and the Source. And that confession is: I AM good, I AM wonderful, I AM loved, I AM accepted, I AM of worth and value, I AM powerful, I AM one with the Divine, I AM blessed, I AM grateful for this moment, I AM one with Christ, I AM enough, I AM prosperous, I AM wise, I AM complete, I AM a gift of God. I encourage you to read appendix three at the end of the book, which has 100 I AM affirmations for daily living to help you reprogram your thinking and what you confess each day. Use these affirmations daily and see the change that can occur over time.

Why is this important? Because what you think and then say impacts the quantum field of energy and draws that energy vibration to you. It can be no other way. Say enough negative low-vibration confessions, and it will manifest in your life. Even worse is confessing lies about yourself and your life situation, not the truth as the Divine sees it. Your situation may feel hopeless, but you are not hopeless; you are complete in the Source of all life. There is a significant difference. "I feel hopeless" is expressing your feelings, which is valid. "I am a hopeless case" is a lie. You are not a hopeless case. Confessing lies will damage your life and limit your future.

I cannot tell you how crucial this is. Practicing positive, true affirmations about myself, what I can do, and what I have, in agreement with the Source of all life, has dramatically impacted my thinking and life.

In 2019, I began expressing gratitude for being an author and completing and publishing all my books. At that time, I had never authored a book or published anything. But I confessed it as though it was already done. I confessed that I was a great writer and that each book was published. I could see them in my mind and imagined myself signing books for those who had purchased them. I confessed this every day and gave thanks it was true. Today, I have published three books, with more on the way. That is the power of *homologeo*.

All I did was agree with what the Spirit had shown me in meditation and contemplation. I agreed with that reality as though it was completed and confessed it. This is how we are intended to live. Would you be willing to take a small step and confess the affirmations at the end of this book? Would you believe that they are true of you at this moment? Would you be open to beginning to meditate? To live in the moment? If so, it will be the beginning of an incredible adventure. You will never be the same.

Confess It as Completed

It is easy to ask for things when we do not have them. Our prayers are usually about what we need God to do for us. Or asking Him for things we believe we do not have. This type of prayer is typical and a good beginning point. But it is time to move beyond that to what prayer is: seeing it as already completed. Again, Hebrews 11:1 and Mark 11:24 clearly state that faith is seeing something as completed and agreeing with God that it is. As Jesus said, this type of prayer moves mountains.

There is something powerful about verbal confession. "I love you" has changed many people's lives. That confession can create a new beginning and establish new possibilities. The same can be said of the I AM affirmation discussed in chapter six. When you verbally confess something as true, the quantum field responds as though it is true now. A verbal confession is bringing what is unseen into material form (Hebrews 11:1). Every possible outcome is in potentia, and when we confess that which we have a vision for and can imagine ourselves having, it will, in time, collapse into material form. We do not control when, where, how, or even what it will look like when it does, but be assured it will happen. That is the nature of the quantum field, which is Christ.

Joe Dispenza discusses the idea that the brain does not distinguish between real experiences and those vividly imagined or meditated upon in several of his books and lectures. One of the key texts where he explores this concept in depth is *Breaking the Habit of Being Yourself: How to Lose Your Mind and Create a New One*. Dispenza combines neuroscience, brain chemistry, biology, and quantum physics to explain how thoughts and meditation can change one's brain and reality. He argues that by vividly imagining and emotionally engaging with specific scenarios through meditation, individuals can make measurable changes in their brains, impacting their physical reality.[8]

I admit, it feels a little weird to confess something in the present tense when we do not have it physically. For instance, when practicing this in meditation, I will say, "It is amazing how every cell in my body is healthy." Or "I am so thankful that every cell in my body operates in harmony and balance." I say these things even when I am not feeling good, tired, or have aches and pains. It is my way of directing my brain to see, imagine, and believe that every cell in my body is healthy, whole, and balanced. The brain does not know the difference between your confession, heightened emotion of gratitude and thankfulness, and the actual state of your body or whether it is in hypostasis. It will respond to your visual, emotional, and confessional stimulus. Remember the placebo effect.

The Apostle Paul did this while a prisoner on a ship bound for Rome, to be brought before Caesar.

> *No one had eaten for a long time. Finally, Paul called the crew together and said, "Men, you should have listened to me in the first place and not left Crete. You would have avoided all this damage and loss. But take courage! None of you will lose your lives, even though the ship will go down. For last night an angel of the God to whom I belong and whom I serve stood beside me, and he said, 'Don't be afraid, Paul, for you will surely stand trial before Caesar! What's more, God in his goodness has granted safety to everyone sailing with you.' <u>So take courage! For I believe God. It will be just as he said.</u>"*
> Acts 27:21-25 NLT

Paul confessed that it was a done deal, even if everyone else did not. Can you imagine the rolling of eyes and scoffing that occurred while he was saying this? But that is the difference between a spiritual person and one who lives focused outwardly on current circumstances and the opinions of others.

Confession helps to collapse the wave function in the quantum field into the present moment as a physical reality (remember, every possibility is already true at this moment, as we saw in chapter four). That is faith—agreeing with God and confessing it as already true. That is how you move mountains.

We do not control the ultimate outcome, how it comes about, through whom it comes about, or when it comes about. Our part is to focus with intention, see, imagine, and feel it, and then confess in agreement with the Source of all life that it is done.

A Final Word

Again, this is a warning about the ego (or, as I like to call it, the false ego because your true ego is your soul united in purpose and communion with you as spirit). This false ego has been traumatized, hurt, and disappointed by life, people, and self. It seeks control and cannot be bargained with, placated, or ignored. Confession is not a way to get something material that you hope will help you feel better about yourself, others, or current circumstances. Confession comes from our union in the spirit of Christ, the Source. It comes from meditation and contemplation. It comes from receiving what is already true in the unified energy field through vision. Imagining yourself in it as though it is already done. Producing deep feelings of gratitude and thankfulness. Then, confessing boldly, it is already yours. It finds its origin in the spirit, and it manifests eventually in the physical world. This manifestation is always based on love for oneself and others. Seeking the highest interest of everyone is agape love.

Do not confuse a wounded soul longing for something external to heal it, for a vision given through inward communion with the Source of all life, and with confidence, boldly confessing it as completed, present tense. This is living from within. This is a life that thrives.

Chapter 9

Manifesting in the Five Percent

The state of your life is nothing more than a reflection of the state of your mind.

Wayne Dyer

Based on our discussions in chapters three and four, this world is not what it appears to be. Everything is energy. All energy is in vibration and has a frequency. This frequency resonates with and attracts energy of the same frequency and vibration. Physical matter comprises tiny (quantum) subatomic particles that makeup atoms. Billions of atoms make up a molecule. Billions of molecules make up a cell. Billions of cells make up an organ. Organs make up living bodies. And all of it is energy in frequency and vibration.

When we talk about the "5 percent of matter that can be seen and touched," we're referring to the ordinary matter that makes up stars, planets, and everything we interact with daily. This is just a tiny part of the universe, with the rest being dark matter (27%) and dark energy (68%), which we cannot see.

In the context of quantum mechanics, this 5 percent is affected by how particles behave at the quantum level. Particles like electrons or atoms exist in various possible states or locations (the wave function) until we measure them. When we measure them, their wave function collapses, and they settle into a definite state or location that we can see.

Imagine a dark room with an object hidden inside. Before you turn on the light, you know the object is somewhere in the room, but you cannot see it, so it is in multiple possible spots simultaneously. When you turn on the light, you see the object in one specific place. This is similar to how a particle's wave function works: when you measure or observe the particle, it collapses from a cloud of possibilities into a specific state or location.

So, the visible matter we experience results from many particles' wave functions collapsing into specific states when we measure or observe them. Even though tiny particles have numerous possibilities, they end up in specific states or positions when we interact with them.

The whole point of being in this physical life is to raise your vibrations to love, gratitude, thankfulness, joy, generosity, peace, patience, goodness, kindness, gentleness, and self-control (Galatians 5:22, 23).

As you do this in cooperation with the Spirit and focus on what you desire (as one who co-creates with God, see I Corinthians 3:9 and Mark 11:23, 24), the wave function will collapse, and you will manifest that desire in the physical world, which makes up the 5 percent that we can see and touch.

In doing so, you are operating as the spiritual person that you are in Christ. The question is: How can we manifest into this physical world consistently?

Where You Focus Is What You Manifest

Authoring a book is primarily about focus. Most people will never write a book—good for them! It is one of the most time-consuming, complex tasks I have ever undertaken. Writing is simultaneously a source of frustration and satisfaction. How can something be frustrating and satisfying at the same time? Have you ever been married?

It must start with something you feel deeply about and the need to communicate that message. Then, focus on what you want to communicate and the audience that needs to hear it. But what will you write? There is much you could include and not include. First is the research and development of the material itself. Next is writing: typing, correcting, and rewriting. Then there is final editing and the book's internal and external design.

That means while you are focused on authoring a book, there are many other worthy things you are not focused on. This is called opportunity costs. You give up the ability to focus on other things you could accomplish so you can focus on writing and finishing the book. However, the more you focus with intention and imagine the book as already written and completed, with feelings of gratitude, the more likely you will see the finished product manifest itself.

Manifesting in the 5 percent of matter we can see and touch is partly why we are in this bodily incarnation. We must learn to raise our inner vibrations of love, peace, joy, gratitude, and thankfulness (also known as fruits of the Spirit) and, in turn, collapse the wave function. But it requires focus. Remember the observer effect from chapter four.

Focusing is difficult in today's world. From cell phones to computers to televisions, the world is screaming for our attention, not to mention emails at work or texts from friends and family. Our brains have been trained to focus for only seconds at a time.

When we meditate, we are not focused on problems or people. We are clearing our minds to the point of thinking nothing. Free of wandering thoughts, we can be in the moment (focus), listen to our spirit (focus), and go inward to the reality of our essence (focus), which is spirit.

The challenge will always be where to focus, and the ego will always try to usurp your best intentions.

Ego and Its Demands

There are three people we must each come to terms with. The first is our negative self-identity based on past traumas, hurts, and disappointments. Because of this negative self-identity, the ego tries to create a second person, the better me, by focusing the soul outwardly. Then, there is your true essence as a spiritual soul-being.

This spiritual soul-being is powerful and wonderful and has never been less than, or needed to improve anything. You are in union with the Source of all life, and everything you need lives within you now. But your wounded and traumatized ego does not accept that and always wants to direct you outwardly away from your inner spiritual essence.

Ego always stands in the way of living in the moment, enjoying who you are as a spiritual being, and manifesting the life you desire in the 5 percent.

In Figure 9.1, we see an illustration of this problem. The ego wants to focus you outwardly, searching for an answer to the inward trauma, hurts, and disappointments that have created a negative self-identity, hoping that somehow people, things, achievements, power, and money can solve these inward issues. Looking inwardly to your true spirit self is unacceptable to the ego, and it will try to thwart you at every turn. Therefore, the ego wants to look outward and focus on those things outside yourself to solve the problems it believes are critical.

In meditation on your spirit, focusing inwardly endangers the ego's control and desire to manipulate everything. Because of this negative self-identity, the ego keeps trying and struggling to become, to be, someone. To solve all the problems through self-effort. But it never works. There is always one more problem and negative identity to deal with, and ultimately, it leaves you feeling exhausted, overwhelmed, and defeated.

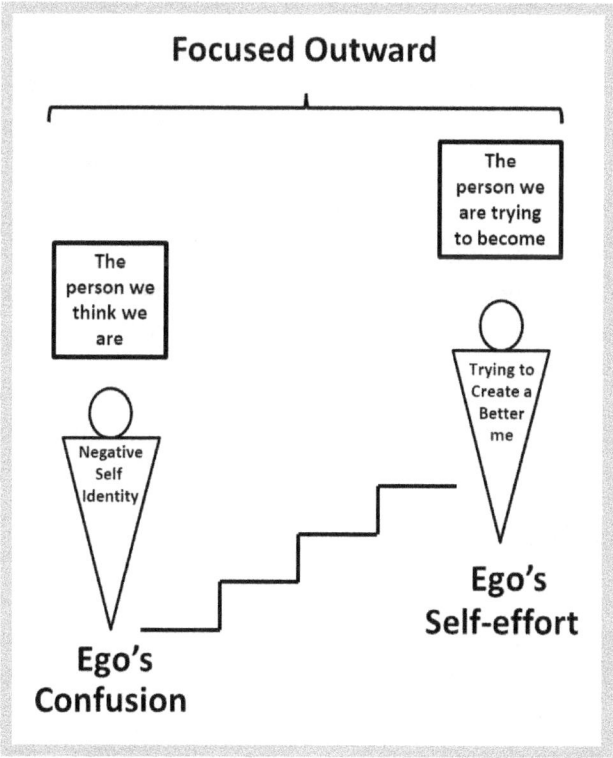

Figure 9.1 The ego constantly wants to focus us outward due to a negative self-identity created by past traumas, hurts, and disappointments. The ego's confusion drives us to make ever-increasing efforts to solve this negative self-identity by looking

outward at people, things, money, power, and position in the hope of feeling better about ourselves.

The ego will attempt to keep you focused outward each time you seek to focus inward on your spirit and union with the Divine Life. People have called this the monkey brain. Think of when a monkey is excited and all over the place. Our brain does that because it is uncomfortable with silence, non-activity, and conscious focus.

A client I worked with was frightened of silence, non-activity, and focusing inwardly. She did not like being alone with herself and her thoughts. Having people around, with activity and the noise that goes with it, was much more comfortable than focusing inwardly, listening, and being quiet and present in the moment. This was her ego's way of avoiding difficult things that she was uncomfortable with (especially unresolved traumas and hurts from the past) and maintaining control. Control is the one thing the ego must have because it believes that with control, pain can be avoided. But this is an illusion.

What is the way out? Recognizing and enjoying the flow of the Spirit.

Life in Spirit Is Like a River: Get in the Flow

I rafted the Colorado River with some friends some years ago. This was my first time on a raft or a river, for that matter. They were experienced at rafting and invited me to join them. We reviewed all the safety measures, my responsibility, and where I would sit on the raft. They showed me how to use my paddle and work as a team on the river. The one thing they warned me about was the power of the river. It was important not to fight it but to work with it, one with its flow and control. Do not fear the river; respect it and practice self-awareness when in it. The river moved slowly at times, and we could enjoy talking and taking it easy. Other times, it became steeper and rougher and required our full attention. When we hit the rapids, I experienced its tremendous force and flow, but also the fact that if I moved with the river and did not fight it, it would do the work. I could enjoy the full power, flow, and movement, which required less energy and effort. Somehow, I felt one with the river and its constant flow.

Life in the Spirit is like a river: You can flow with it or swim against the current. Most people prefer maintaining the illusion of control and swimming against the current rather than going with the flow and letting the river's power move them forward.

Swimming against this spiritual current is exhausting and needs more significant energy expenditure the longer you do it. The entire universe is part of this spiritual reality. It was created in love to respond to your observation. Entering the flow of the Spirit is the pathway to inner rest and peace. The path to raising your vibrations and manifesting naturally in the 5 percent It is part of your purpose for living. Jesus was a spiritual person who lived in the flow of the Spirit.

It is the spirit who gives life; the flesh profits nothing. The words that I speak to you are spirit, and they are life.
John 6:63 NKJV

He emphasized spirit over the efforts of the flesh or ego. The efforts of ego profit nothing. He then pointed out His words are "spirit, and they are life." This is the importance of living in the flow of the Spirit: what you think and say either produces life (from the Spirit) or is destructive (from the ego).

However, the helper, the Holy Spirit, whom the Father will send in

> *my name, will teach you everything. He will remind you of everything that I have ever told you.*
> John 14:26 GW

The inner spirit is the focal point for all wisdom and understanding, not outward things or people. The Spirit, or helper (the word in Greek is *paraclete*, meaning "one who comes alongside to help"), is the one we flow with and listen to in the spiritual river. And everything you need lives within you.

> *He who believes in Me, as the Scripture has said, out of his heart will flow rivers of living water.*
> John 7:38 NKJV

The Spirit within every person is described as a flowing river. But to get into that flow, one must believe, which could be translated as *confident trust*. We must begin to trust our spirit within us, listen to it, and do so confidently. One must give oneself to that inner flow in confident trust, let go, and enjoy the power and direction of the spiritual river within you. The inner life, living from within, from spirit, is a life that thrives!

The Apostle Paul also stressed living in the power of this spiritual river that is within us.

> *When we tell you these things, we do not use words that come from human wisdom. Instead, we speak words given to us by the Spirit, using the Spirit's words to explain spiritual truths. But people who aren't spiritual can't receive these truths from*

God's Spirit. It all sounds foolish to them and they can't understand it, for only those who are spiritual can understand what the Spirit means. Those who are spiritual can evaluate all things, but they themselves cannot be evaluated by others. For, "Who can know the LORD's thoughts? Who knows enough to teach him?" But we understand these things, for we have the mind of Christ.
I Corinthians 2:13-16 NLT

Living from this river within us means we listen to the inner words of the Spirit and understand spiritual truths. This is life in the flow of the spiritual river. However, those who do not live that way, which is most people, do not understand the things of the inner spirit. It is foolish to them to meditate and be in the moment, to listen in quietness to one's inner spirit. They do not understand because they are not attuned to the Spirit that lives in them. Spiritual people who flow with the river within them can understand spiritual things. They can understand at a spiritual level. Those who live from ego, focused outwardly, cannot fully understand, or judge a spiritual person. You can live from your spirit and know the things of the Spirit because you (and everyone) have Christ's mind living within you. Everything you need lives within you at this moment.

Many mystics from different faiths have written about this inner life. Rumi, the thirteenth-century Persian poet and Sufi mystic, wrote,

When you do things from your soul, you feel a river moving in you, a joy.[1]

Abraham Isaac Kook (1865-1935), a Jewish mystic, writes,

The inner soul of a person is the main thing, and the external person and his behavior are secondary.[2]

In a paraphrase from the Tao Te Ching, by Laozi,

Life is a series of natural and spontaneous changes. Don't resist them – that only creates sorrow. Let reality be reality. Let things flow naturally forward in whatever way they like.

The Gospel of Thomas is a non-canonical text that contains sayings attributed to Jesus. It is part of what is known as the Nag Hammadi library, discovered in Egypt in 1945. These are likely Gnostic scriptures that had been hidden away for centuries. The text is interesting for its lack of narrative; instead, it comprises 114 sayings of Jesus, some of which resemble those found in the New Testament, while others are unique to this gospel. One text brings out the reality of the Spirit of Christ within us,

Jesus said, "It is I who am the light which is above them all. It is I who am the all. From me did the all come forth, and unto me did the all extend. Split a piece of wood, and I am there. Lift up the stone, and you will find me there."[3]

This Gnostic text emphasizes the union of all things in Christ. The flow of the Spirit, the river, is Christ Himself and can be found in all things, as all things are in Him.

Before you accuse me of pantheism, consider that all things are in Christ, yet they are not Christ. I am in Christ, yet I am not Christ. This is the mystery of union, yet it is true.

The log ride (or log flume) was one of my favorite amusement park rides as a kid. The fiberglass logs would float in the rushing water, around curves, down slides into pools of water, splashing the participants with water and anyone walking nearby. I was always fascinated by the enormous amount of water it took to keep the logs moving without getting stuck. The only requirement of the participants was to sit back, relax, and enjoy the ride. That is an example of the torrent of living water (Spirit) within you, just waiting for you to sit back, relax, and enjoy the river's flow. Everything is done in Christ; there is nothing to add or work up. Would you be willing to flow with this inner life of spirit and enjoy the ride?

Manifest Spiritually or Work to Produce?

Working smarter, not harder, is a saying I have heard since college. For instance, some salespeople will schedule their day in specific blocks of time. A block dedicated to calling on *targeted* potential leads, a block of time to follow up on *qualified* prospects, and a block to close *confirmed* orders. This way, they make money by *consistently* adding to the sales pipeline, *proactively* moving it forward, and *effectively* closing deals. They work smarter, not harder.

Marketing professionals have discovered that targeting the right audience leads to significant cost savings and improved sales efficiency. Crafting the right message for the right platform—one that resonates with the target audience—is essential for boosting sales. By focusing on proper targeting and selecting the right platform, they can work smarter, not harder.

Leaders can waste time in meetings with people who are not directly tied to the leaders' ability to move the organization forward based on their vision and goals. Effective leaders have learned to spend more time with fewer people to leverage their effectiveness and potential organizational impact. An effective leader knows how to work smarter, not harder.

Can the same be said of living spiritually? Yes! Based on the things we have discussed in Part two of this book, it is a question of moving from an outward focus of doing to an inward spiritual focus that leads to an outward manifestation, which, in time, will entail doing. The more we focus outwardly, the greater the work and energy expended and the less we accomplish. The more we focus inwardly, the more we manifest outwardly, with much less effort and energy.

This is not only a mindset change but also a change in how we define work. Work is first internal, in the Spirit, which means the focus must be internal. Meditation is a good first step to help in this transition.

But the ego will not simply sit back and let you do that. It wants to control, manipulate, and have something to do outwardly. When we work hard, endorphins are released, and they help us feel good. Outward work and effort have a physiological benefit. However, this work and effort should be secondary to the internal focus, with intention, vision, imagination, intense emotion of gratitude, and confession that should accompany it.

Once the inner work is done, life comes to you naturally, and the outward work becomes evident and empowering. What, when, where, and how this manifests in the outward world is none of your business. Leave that in the hands of the Source of all life. The most challenging part is not controlling these things. Jesus put it this way,

> *If any of you want to be my follower, you must give up your own way, take up your cross, and follow me.*
> Mark 8:34b NLT

This verse has many applications, but I want to look at it from the vantage point of living from your spirit in union with Christ. This means the ego or self will feel like it is dying. He describes this feeling of death in terms of crucifixion, which was a slow, agonizing death and usually took three to four days for the victim to die. That means this is a process, and it can feel uncomfortable as we make the transition. Only then can we live from our inner life. This is the way of Jesus, which is the way of the inner spirit.

We can continue trying, doing, and expending tremendous energy to create the desired results. Or we can live in the flow of the spiritual river within us and see life come to us naturally, providing opportunities at the right place and time. This is a life that thrives, not just survives. It is the inner way of the Spirit.

However, the great challenge is the transition we go through in living this inner way, which is the topic of part three of this book.

Part Three

Live from Within: The Transition

Chapter 10

Everything You Need Is Within You

Our thoughts and imagination are the only real limits to our possibilities.

Orison Swett Marden

A farmer was walking down the road and came upon a beggar. The beggar asked the farmer for something to eat, and the farmer responded, "I have little myself due to a poor harvest, and you ask me for something to eat?" And he walked on. Later, a merchant walked by, and the beggar asked him for money. The merchant responded, "I must manage money responsibly, and I only have so much. Giving to you, one who is obviously irresponsible is not something I can do." And the merchant walked on. Later, a billionaire dressed in expensive clothing walked by, and the beggar asked him for any piece of clothing he could spare, as the day was cold. The billionaire looked at the beggar's coat he was wearing and asked him where he got it. The beggar responded, "I found it in an alleyway near a dumpster. The owner had abandoned it." The wealthy man smiled at the beggar and said, look in the inside pocket hidden in the left side of the coat. The beggar, hoping the man might help him, did as he asked, found the hidden pocket, and looked in it. And there, to his amazement, was a clip of 50 $100 bills. The beggar, in astonishment, asked, "How did you know the coat had the money clip inside it?" The wealthy man responded, "Because that is my coat that a thief stole several days ago and later abandoned, not knowing what was in the hidden inner pocket." The wealthy man gazed intently at the beggar and said, "You already had everything you needed inside the coat. Keep the coat and money clip as my gift and enjoy the abundance that is yours already."

The parable has many things to teach us about the inner way of spirit that leads to a thriving life.

- The beggar represents all of us who live perpetually with an attitude of lack, looking outward as though we have no inward resources. The beggar looked to others who also lived with this same mindset. This is the loop that keeps us from thriving from our inner spirit.
- The farmer was like the beggar in attitude: *"I have little myself."* He looked outward at the poor harvest, saw himself as one with little, and would not give food to someone hungry. Yet the farmer had dedicated his life to producing food for people and experienced plentiful harvests. The farmer was focused outward and lived in a mindset of lack and scarcity.
- The merchant was also like the beggar in attitude: *"I only have so much."* He considered his outward provisions of money and assets insufficient. Like the farmer, the merchant focused outward and lived in a mindset of lack and scarcity. He also judged the beggar by outward appearances, not knowing that the beggar had all he needed, but did not realize it.

- The billionaire represents the Source of all life, who directs us to the inner hidden resources we are unaware of. The beggar had not taken the time to examine the coat thoroughly. Otherwise, he would have discovered the money clip. The billionaire, in love and grace, looked at the confused beggar and gave him the coat and the money clip freely. We too have been given everything we need as a gift, and it lives in the hidden place of our spirit in union with the Divine Life.

Living from within requires changing how we see ourselves: from a beggar looking outward to one who is wealthy inward, a powerful spiritual being. This results in a mindset change from lack, scarcity, and selfishness to completeness, abundance, and generosity. You are a powerful spiritual being in the Divine Life, with all the abundance of Christ within you. This chapter explores how you transition to the inner way and discover the wealth already there, like the beggar in the parable, so you can enjoy a life that thrives, not just survives.

Everything Is Energy

As a reminder, I want to emphasize that everything is energy. The chair you sit on, the table you eat at, the car you drive, the bed you sleep in, and the clothes you wear are all energy, as is the body you live and experience life in. It is energy that has collapsed into a dense material form that can be seen, touched, and held. Most energy cannot be seen. This energy moves at a very high vibration and cannot be seen in the portion of the electromagnetic spectrum our eyes can see, but it is just as valid as the energy that makes up the matter you can see, touch, and feel.

Einstein's formula of special relativity, $E=MC^2$, states that energy equals mass times the speed of light (186,000 miles per second) squared. Therefore, a tiny amount of mass (matter) equals an enormous amount of energy. Energy and mass are the same thing.

What are the implications for living from within, from the spirit-person you are? It means that you are a very powerful person, you are more than you ever dreamed possible, and the possibilities are endless.

It means everything you need as a spirit-being of energy lives within you. You need never see yourself as the beggar did, inadequate or less than what is required. You can, as Paul wrote,

Do all things through Christ who strengthens me.
Philippians 4:13 NKJV

You can move mountains as Jesus taught because it is in the nature of your higher spiritual self to do so (Mark 11:23). You can do more extraordinary things than Jesus did because, as a powerful spiritual energy-being, it is in your nature to do so (John 14:12). Nothing is impossible in that union and energy that is your life. The question is: Will you embrace the spiritual energy-being you are as the essence of who you are?

Embracing Your Essence: Spirit Energy

The pop song "Material Girl" by Madonna was released in 1984 and was a significant hit that helped propel her to stardom and established her as a music icon. The song acknowledges society's growing focus on material things, especially money. It was a provocative commentary on society's misguided priorities. I remember listening to the music on my car radio and thinking, "That is the truth; we are a society that is focused on material things to the detriment of things that matter, such as relationships and spirituality." We focused on temporary material things and forgotten our authentic essence as powerful spiritual beings.

As we discussed, at your core, you are a spirit entity made of energy, as all things are energy. You have a unique spirit-soul, and you are experiencing a human life (body). The body is characterized by its attributes (tall, short, fast, slow, strong, weak, athletic, or uncoordinated), abilities (talents, intelligence, and skills), and senses (smell, touch, sight, taste, and hearing). The soul comprises thinking (mind), feelings (emotions), and behavior (will). The ego resides in the soul and is expressed in the conscious self. It is what the Apostle Paul called the "flesh." Remember, the ego is driven by fear and a desire to avoid pain and enhance personal gain and pleasure through controlling and manipulating people, things, and circumstances. It cannot be bargained with, reformed, or redeemed. It must go through a reduction, or death, as Paul described it (Galatians 5:24), so that the higher spiritual self, who you really are as a spiritual energy-being, can manifest itself. Figure 10.1 illustrates this.

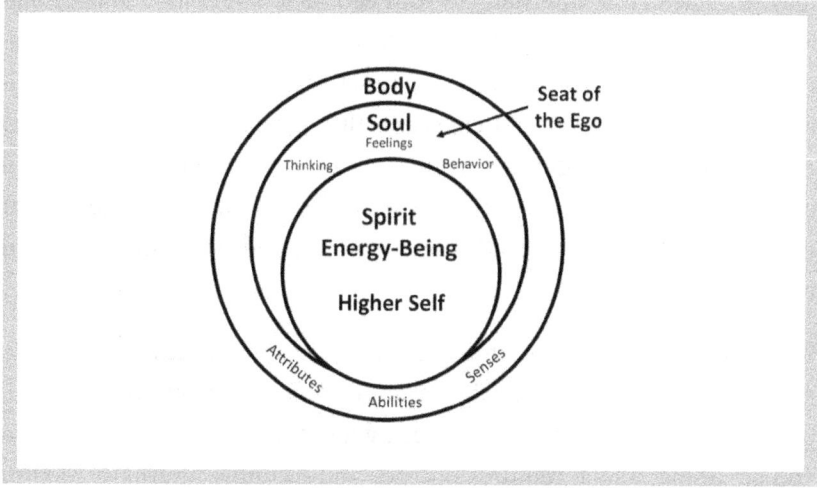

Figure 10.1 You are a spirit energy-being, your higher self, one with your unique soul. This is represented by your ability to think, feel, make choices (behavior), and experience a human life in a body characterized by specific attributes and abilities, and guided by the five senses.

An exercise I use with my ego has helped me over the years. I have an internal conversation with my ego from the place of my spirit or higher self. Ask your higher self to make you aware of how you feel, what you are thinking, and what you are doing or about to do. The ego works from fear, anxiety, desire for control, or other desires. When you become aware of how you feel, such as fear, or what you think, for instance, "I am not enough", that is an opportunity to gently deal with your ego about who is in charge. The goal is to let the ego know you have heard the fears, concerns, and desires. You are not ignoring them. Then, let the ego know that your higher self (the adult you) is in charge and will care for the ego's concerns and the well-being of the body. Tell the ego to be quiet and only observe. The higher self will handle the concerns at the appropriate time and in the appropriate way.

You must develop this skill. It will initially feel clumsy and weird. You may struggle to talk internally to your ego, as it is very loud and strong-willed. The goal is to be gentle and redirect the ego to one of observation, not participation. As you practice this, you will have some failures, which are typical and expected. But, if you are consistent, new neural pathways will develop in time, and the conscious ego will begin calming down. Remember, your focus is on your higher self, your union with the Source of all life, and living and operating from that reality, not your ego.

Reduction of the ego in this manner over time is less distressing, gentler, and results in more significant change. It also builds your skill of greater awareness of how you feel, what you are thinking, and what you are doing, which requires practice and listening internally to your higher self.

The key to thriving, not just surviving, is living from within, from your higher self, the spirit energy-being you are. The key to living from within is to embrace the true you, a spirit energy-being that is one with the Source of all life. Accepting this at the heart of who you are is non-negotiable. It is one of the most challenging things in life because it threatens the ego and its control. Take it from me, it demands to be in control!

A woman I was working with at this point in the spiritual coaching process said, "I hear what you are saying, but I am afraid of losing myself and who I am if I go down this path." This is the primary fear for many. If I lose the brand I have created, the reputation I have worked on, and the image I have meticulously built, then who will I be? This is a significant obstacle in the age of social media. But none of these things is who you are. It is like a mirage that lasts for a little while and is gone. But it is the false person that the ego desperately wants to save.

Living from within, from your higher self, is how to thrive and genuinely enjoy life. The longer-term answer to your transition, however, is alignment.

Aligning Your Spirit, Soul, and Body

Achieving optimal health relies on a harmonious balance between diet, exercise, and lifestyle choices. Each element plays a crucial role, and their alignment ensures they support rather than undermine each other.

- *Diet* provides the essential nutrients, vitamins, and minerals that the body needs to function correctly.
- *Exercise* is equally important. Regular physical activity strengthens the heart, muscles, and bones, improves mental health, and helps regulate weight.
- *Lifestyle choices* encompass other aspects such as proper sleep, stress management, and avoiding harmful habits like smoking or excessive alcohol consumption. Quality sleep is vital for

recovery and overall health, while stress management techniques such as mindfulness and relaxation exercises can mitigate the negative impacts of chronic stress.

A well-rounded approach ensures that diet provides the necessary fuel for exercise. When diet, exercise, and lifestyle choices align, they work synergistically to enhance health and prevent disease.

The same is true for manifesting externally. Since everything you need already lives within you, your focus should be aligning the body and soul with the higher self. Many people live with their body and soul out of alignment with their higher self, and the results are evident: anxiety, fear, worry, moodiness, control issues, and other egoic responses. Unresolved tension, stress, and fear impact the body and its ability to operate in homeostasis.[1]

Alignment occurs as we focus on the moment, on the inner spirit, or higher self, and begin to listen, visualize, imagine, feel gratitude, and confess in harmony with the higher self. The soul operates at its highest capacity and wholeness when it aligns with the higher self, as seen in Figure 10.2.

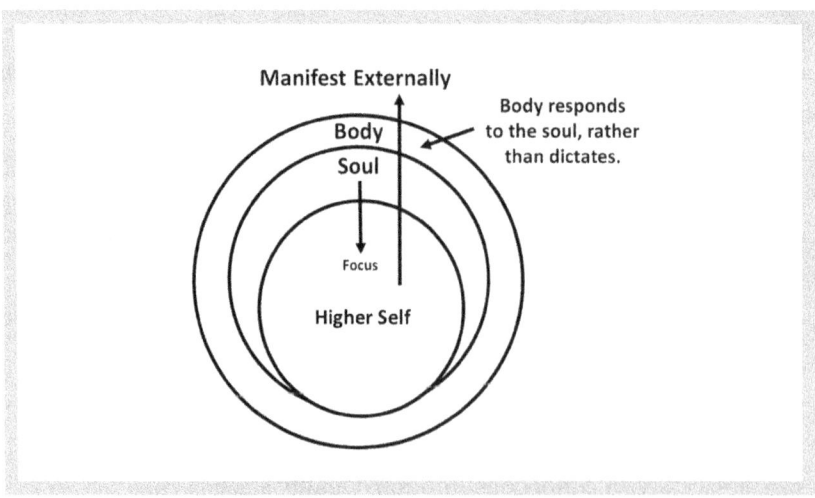

Figure 10.2 When the soul focuses on the spirit, or higher self, the soul and spirit align in purpose and action. In time, the body responds and comes into alignment, which promotes external manifestation from the higher self through the soul.

This alignment starts with focusing in the moment through meditation or mindfulness where there is no time, no place, and no one: just the moment. The point where spirit, soul, and body are united in focus, purpose, and action. (We will examine the practical aspects of meditation and contemplation in chapter twelve).

We can contemplate what we want to manifest as we focus in the moment. These things come from intuitively listening to our higher self, which is in union with the Source of all life. As we listen, we will know what to focus on, come to visualize it, and then imagine it as already done. But how do I listen to the Spirit?

As with everything we have talked about, this is a developed skill. Initially, we must listen actively to our spirit with conscious awareness. Eventually, listening becomes more natural, and we are unaware we are doing it.

This listening is like the still, small voice Elijah heard (I Kings 19:11, 12). This voice cannot be heard in the hurry and bustle of daily life if you have not disciplined yourself to listen. It is difficult to hear if your focus is on material things. Your goal is to be *involved* with material things but *focused* on your higher self. We all have relationships, jobs, and responsibilities in this life that must be addressed. However, it is possible to be involved with these outward things while focusing on our inner higher self. As the Apostle Paul wrote,

> *Never stop praying.*
> I Thessalonians 5:17 NLT

Learning to listen to your higher self continuously is possible.

Traditional prayer is a good starting point, but the goal is to transition to meditative listening. This transition means talking less and meditating more. Telling the Source of all life what you need is fine, but it is better to listen to your spirit when you realize that everything you need lives within you in union with the Source. As we practice listening more, receiving becomes more natural and asking less necessary. This is the alignment of spirit, soul, and body.

Thank your higher self for assisting and guiding you in aligning your spirit, soul, and body. The Spirit will help you in this process and give you the guidance needed each moment.

Humility and receptivity are essential and will protect you as you go on this journey. And with this, an open mind. *Closed-mindedness is the enemy of all spiritual progress.* A cursory review of Jesus' life and Paul's writings clarifies this.

Experience, Learn, Love

The reality is that everything you need lives within you. This freedom allows you to enjoy your experiences without fear and learn through them. When you can do this, these experiences are of great value in this incarnation, and you grow in higher vibrations of love and gratitude as you learn.

We are spirit-soul beings living in a human body and having a human experience. Every experience is valid. Judging your experience as good or evil is defeating because it limits an open mind through which personal growth can be realized.

Most of my clients struggle with judging the past or condemning themselves for perceived wrongdoing or poor decisions. They find it difficult to forgive themselves and bemoan wandering off the "narrow path."

They fail to realize that every experience leads to the next experience, and, like a tapestry, it is incomplete without the perceived wrongdoings or poor decisions. All of it is needed and valuable in your journey of learning and growing. God judges none of it, but He is using all of it for your good.

In college and attending business school, I prepared for tests by memorizing formulas, practicing problems, and learning concepts I knew would be tested. When I did poorly on a test, I looked at the graded test to see how the problems should have been solved so I could learn from my mistakes. This helped me learn to solve the problems correctly on the next test and improve my overall grade. For someone like me who struggled with self-loathing, being down on myself was natural. I had to learn that everything could work to my benefit if I would let it. The question was not the grade of the last test. The question was: Am I willing to learn from my mistakes, incorporate those lessons, and improve the next time? Judging myself is a pointless exercise. Learning from my mistakes, loving myself, and moving on is much more productive.

There are many different experiences from which we can learn and grow. Every experience is valid if we are willing to learn from it. I did not say every experience is pleasant, pleasurable, or easy. As I write this, I am experiencing nerve pain from a chronic illness. "Why don't you just use your meditation and contemplation practices to heal it," you might ask. I do, and it helps tremendously. But that does not mean the nerve pain does not serve my highest good. "How can pain and suffering be for your highest good?" I do not fully understand this, but I have learned that pain and suffering often help me to learn and grow in this life. I do not seek or desire it, but it has been a tool God can use for good.

Being open-minded, living in the love of the Spirit rather than religious fear, and seeing each moment as a gift helps us grow. This growth is achieved by learning to live from within rather than focusing outward. As we live from within, from our spiritual energy, we learn to love ourselves as we are. Loving ourselves with compassion, empathy, and gentleness is a growth process.

Most of my clients have various things in common. Firstly, they are caught in a cycle of self-loathing and shame, which manifests every time we visit. How can you grow and learn to love yourself and others when caught in self-loathing and shame? It is like being in a cage with no exit.

Secondly, they believe lies about themselves that keep them in a cage of self-loathing and shame. "There is something wrong with me" and "I am unlovable" are the two lies about their identity they struggle with the most.

How do we escape these lies? By learning that our authentic essence is our higher self within us and that we are worthy of love, respect, compassion, and empathy. That there is nothing wrong with us and never has been. That we are inherently lovable, made in the image of our creator. But this requires learning to look inward, to our spirit to find the truth of our essence, not outward to what society, religion, or people say.

Learning to love ourselves is the primary purpose of our incarnation on this planet. Loving ourselves opens the door to loving others rather than using or fearing them.

Love your neighbor as yourself.
Galatians 5:14b NLT

We can engage them as individuals worthy of love, respect, empathy, and compassion. We may not agree with their behavior, choices, opinions, or lifestyle. But none of that is essential to love someone, just as they are, created by God and worthy of love.

However, there are specific outward gravitational forces that must be overcome so that you can begin living from within. That is the focus of our next chapter.

Chapter 11

Living from Within

What lies behind us and what lies before us are tiny matters compared to what lies within us.

Henry David Thoreau

We cannot teach people anything; we can only help them discover it within themselves.

Galileo Galilei

Escape velocity is the minimum speed an object needs to break free from the gravitational pull of a planet or other celestial body and move into space without further propulsion. Imagine you are trying to jump out of a deep hole. To escape, you must jump high enough to overcome the hole's walls and not fall back in it. Similarly, escape velocity is the "jump" speed required for an object to overcome a planet's gravity and not fall back. For Earth, this speed is about 11.2 kilometers per second or roughly 25,000 miles per hour. If an object or spacecraft can reach this speed, it can escape Earth's gravity and continue traveling through space without additional propulsion. In essence, escape velocity is the speed at which an object's moving energy (kinetic) is enough to counteract the gravitational energy pulling it back.

The same can be said for living from within, focused on your higher self, your spirit-soul. To do so, you must reach escape velocity, or you will continue to fall back into living focused on the outward material world and out of alignment with your spirit.

This chapter examines the outward challenges that act as a gravitational pull to keep you from reaching escape velocity so you can consistently live from your higher self. We also examine what is required to break free of these forces and the change in how we see ourselves in relation to these forces individually.

Jesus said it this way,

> *I assure you and most solemnly say to you, unless a grain of wheat falls into the earth and dies, it remains alone [just one grain, never more]. But if it dies, it produces much grain and yields a harvest.*
> John 12:24 AMB

The ego must undergo a reduction, a setting aside, that can feel painful. We looked at this in the last chapter. The same is true for focusing on outward things that have gravitationally held us over time.

But, as we release these things, we break free and begin to enjoy the spiritual freedom that has always been ours in the Divine Life.

Gravitational Forces

Innumerable things function as opposing gravitational forces, keeping us from focusing inwardly on our spirit. We experience life in a human body operating in the natural world of matter. We need food, security, clothes, shelter, a job to provide money, a family to love us, a sense of fulfillment, and so on.

In this process, this world of matter fools us into believing and feeling it is Reality (big R). But it is spirit, the unseen energy, which is the big R Reality. The physical matter we interact with is temporary and will fade away. Energy has collapsed into matter, physical form, but it is not the greater reality. It is like a Broadway play with other actors playing parts as we play our part, experiencing life, learning, and growing. Our part in this play is to learn to focus inward on spirit, our higher self, and manifest outward into this material world.

To do this, we must break free of the gravitational forces of people and things that keep us focused on this external world.

In this instance, think of kinetic energy (moving energy) as the degree to which we focus inwardly in meditation and contemplation. The greater the focus, the more kinetic energy builds to the point that it overcomes the gravitational forces attracting our focus outward. But it is difficult for the soul to be pulled from the gravitational forces that have been its main source of meaning and fulfillment for so long. It is a reduction process for the ego. Christ and our union in Him, our higher self, must be our focus, not our ego.

He must become greater and greater, and I must become less and less.
John 3:30 NLT

The higher self must receive greater attention, focus, and energy, while the ego must receive less and less. Some of these gravitational forces can be:

- **Relationships** – those with our spouse, children, parents, or others. When we focus on our inner spirit, those we love will benefit. But not if we make them our focus. It is counterintuitive but true.

- **Possessions** – The pull of material things never ends. Culture and the church hold up the value of home, money, and other possessions. Wealth can be a gravitational pull that is challenging to break free from due to cultural norms and expectations, not to mention the ego's desires.

- **Tyranny of the Urgent** – The call of the important, such as meditation and contemplation, is continually drowned out by the noise and tendency for immediate and seemingly pressing matters to take precedence. Numerous things are *urgent*, but as Jesus said, there is only one essential thing.

But the Lord said to her, "My dear Martha, you are worried and upset over all these details! There is only one thing worth being concerned about. Mary has discovered it, and it will not be taken away from her."
Luke 10:42-43 NLT

Mary discovered that sitting at Jesus's feet and listening to Him (the inner spirit) was of much greater value than the urgency of preparing a meal. There is time for both, but one is more important than the other. Have you discovered it as Mary did?

- **Problems** – Trouble and problems are part of life; overcoming them is part of our existence in our earthly incarnation. But we can be obsessed with difficulties to the point they are all we think about and focus on. The more we focus on a problem, the less likely we are to overcome it. But the more we go inward to our spirit and union in the Divine, the more potential solutions and answers will come *to us*.

- **Physical Needs** – Every person needs food, water, shelter, clothing, and security. If you are homeless and without these things, talking about living from within seems meaningless. Even when our basic needs are met, they are always at the top of our minds. These needs carry a strong gravitational force to keep the mind focused outward and the emotions in a place of worry and anxiety, inhibiting living from within.

- **Religion** – This is one of the greatest obstacles to living from within. Organized religion keeps you focused outward because of its demands on its adherents. The list is endless: go to church, work in the church, give to the church, support the building programs, read your Bible, pray, and witness to someone at least weekly. And in your spare time, go on a mission trip out of state or overseas. It is the rare church that focuses its members on their inner life of spirit over all other things.

These are just a few things that keep us from living from within. We have spent our entire lives being trained to live outwardly, and the organized church is one of the worst offenders. But knowing this can help us break free from these gravitational forces.

Most people live one-dimensionally. They are focused on this outer world, unaware of what they think, feel, and do. They are unaware of their spirit, higher self, and what the Spirit wants to reveal to them. They are unaware that an entire unseen world is the big R Reality. Breaking free calls for a change of mind (from ego-dominated to spirit-dominated thinking) regarding this unseen reality, leading to a shift in focus. Once that happens, the gravitational forces that hold us can be broken as we reach escape velocity. But we must first become fully aware of this inner world of spirit, our higher self. With greater understanding, we can engage our higher self and, in time, live consistently at a higher level of spiritual consciousness.

Discovery, Practice, and Skillfulness

Coming into greater awareness initially is like being in a dark room, thinking things are normal until someone turns on a light. It hurts your eyes at first, but in time, you adjust and begin to realize there is much you did not see because of the darkness—much you did not know.

Reaching escape velocity demands this awareness first so you can begin to understand who you are and then consciously engage your spirit. But what is the process of going from being unaware of this reality to unconsciously living in it each moment?

Awareness

Awareness refers to the state or ability to perceive, feel, or be conscious of events, objects, or sensory patterns.[1] At its core, awareness is about being cognizant of something within oneself or one's environment.[2] In this context, we are discussing one's inner spiritual reality.

The old saying, "You don't know what you don't know," is true. There is a transition from being unaware and not knowing to being skilled and consciously engaged. Below is a diagram illustrating this development cycle, which is valid for anything new in our lives.

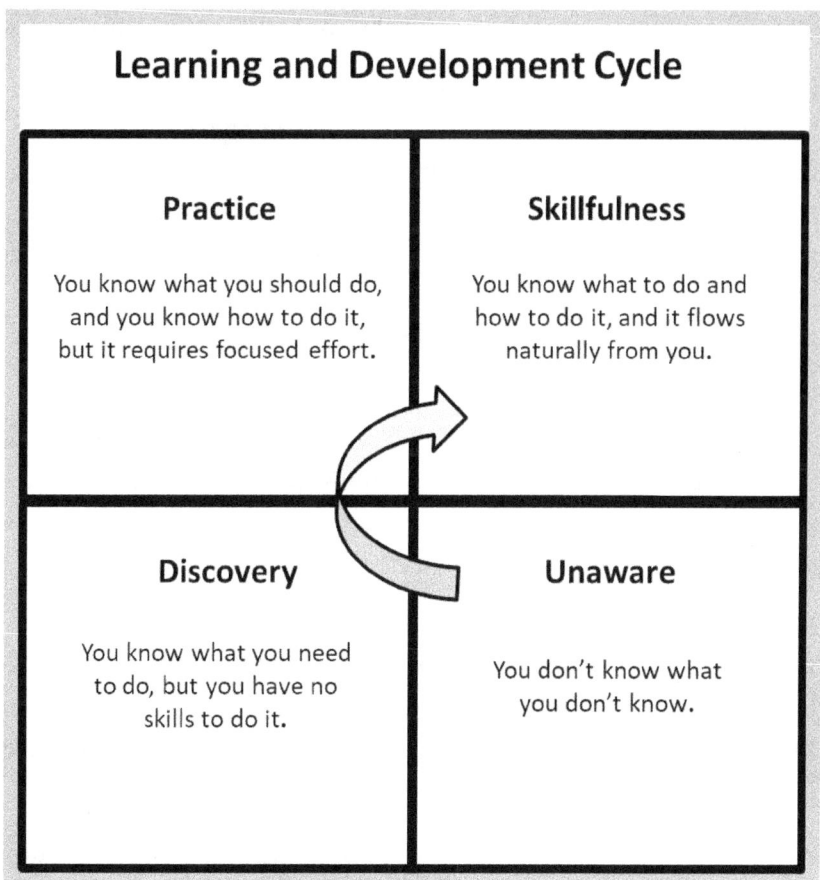

Figure 11.1 The Cycle of Development illustrates how we go from being unaware to discovery, practice, and eventually, skillfulness, which is a higher level of understanding and developed skills. This is a natural process that we go through with anything new.

Discovery of this higher self is the starting point. The ego resists this enlightenment because it threatens its control. Recognizing that you are a powerful spiritual being and that an inward focus is essential could cause the ego to lose this control and sense of safety. Unconscious ignorance is the fate of many, but discovering this makes returning to ignorance impossible.

Many ancient religions and philosophies, including those in Christianity, held that the Earth was the center of the universe, with all celestial bodies orbiting around it. The heliocentric model proposed by Copernicus challenged this belief, later confirmed by Galileo and Kepler, showing that the Earth orbits the Sun, not vice versa. Eventually, religion had to adjust to this reality, but only after the discovery (awareness of the truth) forced the church to do so.

Some ancient cultures and religious traditions believed in a flat Earth. Scientific evidence, including observations from space and the understanding of gravity, has shown that the Earth is not flat but an oblate spheroid.

Some religious interpretations assert that humans were created relatively recently in their present form. Evolutionary biology, supported by extensive fossil evidence and genetic research, demonstrates that humans share a common ancestor with other primates and evolved over millions of years.

Just as these discoveries helped society and religion adjust to the truth, discovering your inner higher self can assist you in focusing on this inner reality. When we are aware that our inner spiritual self is the essence of who we are, we can begin the process of eventually living at a higher level of spiritual consciousness.

Practice

Once we know our inner spirit is our essence and that we should focus inwardly, we need to make changes and practice the skills to do so. You know what to do and how you should do it, but it entails focus and mastering the skills needed to benefit from the power of your inner spirit. We can then begin to practice and build up our skillfulness.

Some might say, "This sounds like work; isn't the Christian life one of grace and resting in the spirit's ability? Are you not teaching the opposite of living by grace?" Yes, life in the Spirit is by grace, in the Spirit's ability. Yet, even Jesus practiced meditation early in the morning before the sun came up (Mark 1:35). Peter went on the roof during the day to pray (Acts 10:9). Paul emphasized the importance of proving yourself as one who handles the scriptures accurately (II Timothy 2:15). It is a matter of personal responsibility to learn the skills that are needed while in this physical world to interact with spirit consistently.

This is the transition from outward to inward focus. We will examine (in chapters twelve and thirteen) how to meditate and control your breathing and mental focus and which thoughts you should focus on. Using this skill, you will learn how to listen to your spirit, know the Spirit's mind, and be guided by it. In time, it will be something you do without even realizing it.

The key to this is repetition. Practicing meditation and contemplation (proactive listening prayer) daily and even each moment so you can naturally live at a higher level of spiritual consciousness. Your activity is now focused inward rather than being outwardly dominated. This is the beginning point of manifesting into the outward world.

Understanding something is different from mastering it. Life in the Spirit and sensitivity to the Spirit are processes that unfold over time. It is a journey of growth and transformation that requires patience and perseverance.

Focusing on outward things is our default setting and what those in this physical world are comfortable with. However, we must shift our focus to our spirit through consistent practice.

Skillfulness

Skillfulness is when we know what we are doing and do it without much effort. We are living at a higher level of spiritual consciousness naturally. Most of the time, we are unaware that we are doing it. This is the goal of life in the Spirit. Living from within becomes the norm rather than the exception (Galatians 5:16; I Corinthians 2:15, 16).

In American baseball, before a batter goes to the plate to try and hit the ball that a pitcher is throwing, he will have spent years developing his ability to see the ball as it is pitched from the pitcher, adjusting his swing to the direction and velocity of the ball, and then hitting the ball with his bat before it passes him. Many hours are spent in batting cages, perfecting this ability. And even with this practice, a hitter is usually only successful 25 percent of the time. "That sounds like failure?" Not in baseball. Many batters hit the ball less than 25 percent of the time. The point is not the failure rate but the willingness to consistently practice and perfect the art of hitting.

Living at a higher level of consciousness is similar. But over time, it becomes our default setting, and intuitively listening to the guidance of our spirit each moment becomes the norm.

Escape Velocity

I had a client who had reached the point in our 'Steps 2 Thriving' program where she was ready to practice meditation and contemplation. We began to practice meditation, starting with breathing exercises, but she struggled. No matter how she tried, she felt overcome by racing thoughts and intense feelings. As we talked, it became clear that controlling her focus was the root of her problem.

The key to breaking this is bringing your focus to as small a point as possible. I suggested she focus on a small area of her body, such as her forehead, neck, chest, or stomach. She chose her forehead. I then asked her to focus on the area of her forehead between her eyes. Then, bring that area down to a tiny dot between her eyes on her forehead. "Can you see that dot on your forehead with your eyes closed?" I asked. "Yes," she responded. "What color is the dot?" "It is purple, a bright purple." "Focus on that small purple dot between your eyes. Watch it grow in brightness and intensity." Now, she was ready to begin the breathing exercise to help her autonomic nervous system and mind slow down. As we practiced the breathing exercises with her focus on the tiny purple glowing dot between her eyes, she began to experience being in the moment; she was now practicing mindfulness.

Mora eventually went on to practice deep levels of meditation and then learned how to transition into contemplation. It took time, as learning any new skill does. Still, she had done the work that helped her make peace with her past, heal the trauma and wounded emotions, and break free of legalism, toxic dogma, and religious people-pleasing. All so she could begin to enjoy living in the moment, listening to her spirit, and enjoying the spiritual inheritance of her union with the Source of all life.

F-O-C-U-S is the key to reaching escape velocity from the outside gravitational forces we deal with. As I wrote earlier, let me know what you *focus on*, and I will tell you your *future outcomes*.

To reach this level of focus means changing your mindset:

- That God is perfect love.
- God loves you perfectly with no conditions.
- You can love yourself just as you are, flaws and all.
- You can experience spiritual freedom as you break free of religious legalism, toxic dogma, and people-pleasing.
- You are empowered from within to love others as equals who are also powerful spiritual beings.

We do not focus on external change. We focus internally, seeking a change of mind first.

As discussed in my previous books, *hamartia*—a Greek word—is the root word for the English word repent. However, it has nothing to do with a change of behavior, as the modern church and society believe. It has to do with a change of mind, a shift in thinking. All change starts with a change of mind, not external efforts to change or do better (what the church has defined as repenting). If you understand this, then making the external shift becomes easier.

As you focus inward, you will intuitively know what to do with complicated relationships. When you focus inward on your spirit in meditation, you will instinctively know what to do with money, houses, cars, and other material objects. And you will realize that is all they are, material objects, there to serve you. But all this requires a change of mindset regarding who you are as a powerful spiritual being and your union with the Source of all life. A change of mindset regarding what should capture your focus, such as mediation and contemplation, and what is secondary, such as external relationships, family, problems, etc.

Everyone can do this, regardless of their personality and behavioral style. Some people are extroverts and people-oriented, but they can change their minds, focus, and practice breathing techniques, leading to more incredible things. Some are introverted thinkers whose minds never stop. Extroverted doers can go from focusing on external doing they think is urgent to living in the moment and focusing on doing what is essential. What you believe will determine the progress you make and the eventual outcomes you manifest. Personal responsibility is vital.

If you are going to reach escape velocity from the outward gravitational forces, then there must be:

- A change of mindset regarding who you are as a powerful spiritual being. Your higher self.

- A shift in focus from outward things to an inward focal point. This allows your autonomic nervous system and body to experience the inner peace and calm already yours as a powerful spiritual being.
- A cultivation of your inner will that leads to outward action to practice this regardless of your unique personality or behavioral style.

Excuses will keep you stuck; changing your mind and focus will eventually empower you to manifest outwardly and begin to thrive!

Letting Go of the Outcomes

We struggle with wanting specific outcomes. The ego wants to control when, where, and how something will happen. But life in the Spirit means letting go of these things.

Most of my clients struggle with letting go of outcomes. They are willing to work with me up to this point and then hit the brakes. "But what if ..." is always the question. Yet, their attempts to control situations, people, and things have resulted in them coming to me for assistance.

We believe there are things we must have; without them, life will never be what we want it to be. This belief leads us to make poor choices and suffer the consequences. A person steals believing they must have the item they are stealing. Someone commits adultery assuming they must have another person in their life. Another remains in a relationship, even if it is abusive, thinking they cannot live without the person. All of these are lies we believe that drive our desire to control and manipulate outcomes.

Living from within frees us of the need to control and manipulate outcomes. The greater our inner awareness and connection to spirit, the less our ego dominates us and the demands for control of outcomes.

Healing from past traumas, hurts, and disappointments is a big help in letting go. If you have not read my book *Alignment of Authentic Love: Living Your Highest Life*, I encourage you to do so. In this book, I walk you through making peace with your past by showing you how to heal from the traumas, hurts, and disappointments that have kept you from spiritual progress. As you heal inwardly, letting go of the demands for specific outcomes becomes more natural.

Knowing you are loved without conditions and never alone in Christ is the most significant help. The Source of all life lives within you and is one with you (John 14:20). You are loved more than you can ever imagine (John 15:9). No matter the outcome, you can always know that you are loved, cared for, and one with Christ. *Love is what overcomes the fears and anxieties of the future and allows you to relax and trust the one who loves you.* In time, you will grow to trust the One who loves you and to know that the outcomes will be what they need to be, at the time they need to be, and in the way they need to be.

Living from within is your spiritual right in Christ. Settle for nothing less. Do not shortchange yourself that which has been gifted to you by grace and is yours this moment.

In the next chapter, we will look at how to do meditation and develop this skill so you can do it as a natural part of your life.

Chapter 12

Engaging Your Higher Self

Meditation practice isn't about trying to throw ourselves away and become something better. It's about befriending who we are already.

Pema Chodron

Meditation profoundly changed my view of spirituality, the meaning of inner peace, and reality itself. Contemplation allowed me to engage my higher self actively. Simply put, meditation calms your mind. Contemplation focuses your mind in a particular direction. Both working together are pathways to higher spiritual consciousness.

When I was first diagnosed with a neurological illness in 2018, I began seeking ways to have greater inner calm, address the chronic anxiety and neurological pain I was experiencing, and increase my ability to focus and concentrate. During this time, I was introduced to meditation practices (mindfulness) and their benefits. I decided to commit myself to this and began studying different meditation types that might suit me.

At first, it was tough to meditate because I was concerned about so many other things. My mind seemed to go a hundred miles an hour, and I was easily distracted. Thoughts were often scattered, and I found it difficult to focus. However, I was determined to make meditation part of my daily routine. In time, my mind began to settle down, and I found it easier to follow my breathing techniques and to focus on my body. This was the beginning of living in the moment, something I had never practiced as a pastor or Christian.

Over the years, I have practiced meditation almost daily and developed my skills and knowledge. It is much easier today to focus than it was when I first began. Christianity tells you to fear so many things, and meditation is one of them. Overcoming that bias and fear was necessary to develop my skill at it.

As I became more comfortable with meditation, I wanted to develop my ability to contemplate in concert with meditation. In the past, I had used scripture to contemplate and enjoyed doing that. But in time, I realized that contemplation should go beyond scripture to a deeper connection with the Spirit of Christ, and thus, my spirit, as we are one. This opened the door to using scripture as a beginning point and listening to the Spirit.

In time, I began to study quantum physics (one of the many studies of general revelation) and the reality of how the universe works at the subatomic scale. The Spirit taught me that we are connected to everything else in this universal energy field, and co-creators with Christ through the observer effect, as we studied in chapter four. This aligned with what scripture taught (I Corinthians 3:9; Mark 11:23) and helped me understand that it is not only a privilege as one who is in union with the Divine but a responsibility to collapse the wave function into material form (Hebrews 11:1). When we collapse the wave function in cooperation with the Spirit we are living as the higher spiritual beings that we are.

In this chapter, we will look at three types of meditation, consider which might be right for you, and explore how to get started. We will consider contemplation in the next chapter.

One might wonder, "I already have a quiet time for prayer and Bible study, so why meditate?" Your existing practices are commendable and should be continued. However, consider meditation and contemplation separate yet equally important parts of your spiritual routine. You could incorporate them into your quiet time or make them the focus of your alone time with God. When combined, scripture, meditation, and contemplation can be spiritually enriching.

Meditation

There are as many ways to meditate as fish in the sea. No one way is correct, but there is a way that works best for you. The key to developing your meditation skills is to find the method you are comfortable with that gives you the most significant results over time. I will provide several options in the next section but encourage you to investigate other methods that might resonate with you (I have included several sources in the resources section).

Meditation is about calming your mind so that you can be in the moment. Whatever meditation method you adopt should help you do this.

Most struggle with staying in the moment. Our minds wander to the past, with regret, resentment, or anger over something someone did to us, or we did to ourselves. Then our minds wander into the future, worried and anxious about things that might happen, or ways we can try to control people, events, or things. Both waste time because we cannot change the past or control the future. Learning to come into the moment is a step of trusting that God lives in the moment, and so should we. If you think about it, moment by moment is all we have, nothing else.

Before starting, you may need to set aside negative messages about meditation from your religious past. Whatever you have been told, Christian mystics have practiced meditation for over 1,900 years, and Catholic monks and other Christian leaders have practiced it for millennia. Set aside any preconceived notions, fears, or biases and open your mind to the possibility of living in the moment.

Once you become more comfortable with your skills, you can meditate at almost any moment of the day. Doing so helps alleviate stress, reduce anxiety, and improve your powers of focus.

Methods of Meditation

Practicing meditation consistently requires finding the method that you are most comfortable with and produces the most meaningful results. In this section, we will look at a few techniques that I have practiced and found helpful. The most important thing is practicing meditation daily to develop your skill level.

Find a quiet place away from people and interruptions. I like to meditate on my patio, but it might be better to do this inside—no cell phones, televisions, computers, or anything that might distract you while you meditate.

Breath and Body Meditation

Breath and body is a form of meditation focused on moving to a state where there are no thoughts, just awareness of your body, breath, and being in the moment. A mental state without active thought allows your brain and body to relax and enjoy inner calm.

How to begin:

Sit relaxed but alert, cross-legged on the floor or a chair or couch with your feet flat on the ground. Keep your back straight and your hands resting on your lap or knees. Avoid lying down, as the body tends to associate this with sleep. Keep good posture during your meditation rather than slumping in the chair. You can play some relaxing meditative music, though it should be focused more on instruments or sounds from nature rather than vocals.

Close your eyes (optional) and breathe deeply through the nose, holding the breath for two seconds, and slowly releasing it through your mouth. Focus on your breathing, noticing the inhale, holding it, and then exhaling. Do this for several minutes, with your focus on the cadence of your breathing. As you breathe, breathe in from your belly rather than your upper body. Let the belly come out as you breathe in.

After a few minutes, continue breathing normally and begin to focus on your body. Start with your head. With your eyes closed, visualize your head and the space it occupies. Then, work down to your shoulders: picture your shoulders and the space they take up. Continue this individually to your chest, stomach, hips, upper legs, knees, lower legs, and feet. When you have completed this, focus on your entire body and visualize it in space at that moment.

Once you reach this point, let your mind focus on your whole body in the present moment. Enjoy the peace and inner calm of no thoughts and nothing but the sound of your breathing as you focus on your body.

When done correctly, this will typically take ten to fifteen minutes. You are now practicing mindfulness, being in the moment.

Concentration Meditation

Concentration meditation, also known as Samatha meditation, is a practice that develops deep concentration and inner tranquility. The word

Samatha means "calm" or "tranquility" in Pali, and the goal of this meditation is to calm the mind by focusing intently on a single object or point of concentration. Over time, this practice leads to profound stillness, mental clarity, and the ability to enter deeper states of meditative absorption.

Common objects of focus include:

- Your Breath: The sensation of the breath entering and leaving the nostrils or the rise and fall of the abdomen.
- A Physical Object: An object, such as a candle flame or a meditation object (like a small statue or mandala).
- A Mantra or Sound: Repeating a word, sound, or phrase mentally or audibly.
- A Mental Image: Visualizing something calming; a peaceful place like a sunny beach or sitting next to a bubbling brook.

The essence of concentration meditation is calming the mind's constant activity by returning attention to the chosen point of focus. When distractions or thoughts arise, you gently bring their attention back to the object without judgment or frustration. The goal is not to suppress thoughts but to allow the mind to settle naturally.

As concentration deepens, the mind becomes more stable and less prone to distractions. This leads to a one-pointed state, where you can remain focused on the object without mental wandering. As concentration develops, you may experience increasingly profound levels of meditative states. These states are marked by deep joy, inner peace, and total absorption in the object of focus.

How to begin:

Sit relaxed but alert, cross-legged on the floor or on a chair or couch with your feet flat on the ground. Keep your back straight and your hands resting on your lap or knees.

Close your eyes (optional) and select an object for concentration, often starting with the breath. If using the breath, pay attention to the sensation of air flowing in and out of your nostrils or the movement of your abdomen. Gently rest your attention on the chosen object, which could be a physical object, a mantra such as "I AM loved," or a mental image of a peaceful place like a flowing brook or waterfall. When your mind wanders, acknowledge the distraction and softly bring your attention back to the object. This process of redirecting attention builds concentration over time.

Distractions like restlessness, drowsiness, or negative thoughts are common, especially at the beginning. It is essential to remain patient and continue bringing attention back to the object.

As focus strengthens, distractions lessen, and the mind begins to quiet down, you may experience feelings of deep tranquility and joy and eventually enter deeper meditative states.

Mindfulness Meditation

The essence of mindfulness meditation is cultivating awareness of the present moment with an attitude of non-judgment and acceptance. It involves paying close attention to one's thoughts, feelings, bodily sensations, and the surrounding environment as they arise without becoming caught up in them or reacting emotionally. It involves accepting whatever arises in your mind without resistance and recognizing it as transient mental events.

The primary focus of mindfulness meditation is to bring your attention fully into the present. You pay attention to what is happening right now, whether it is your breath, body sensations, sounds, or thoughts. This practice helps you stay grounded in the here and now instead of being lost in thoughts about the past or future.

A common anchor for attention in mindfulness meditation is breath. By focusing on the sensation of the breath moving in and out of the body, particularly at the nostrils or the rise and fall of the chest or abdomen, you can anchor your attention and bring yourself back to the present when distractions arise.

Mindfulness encourages an attitude of non-judgment. This means noticing whatever arises in your mind (thoughts, emotions, sensations) without labeling it as good, bad, right, or wrong. You observe with curiosity and openness, accepting whatever is present without resistance.

In mindfulness meditation, you do not try to suppress or eliminate thoughts and emotions. Instead, you observe them as they arise, recognizing them as passing mental events. A core principle of mindfulness meditation is acceptance of what is. Instead of trying to change, resist, or escape from your current experience, you allow things to be as they are. Whether you are feeling uncomfortable, distracted, or calm, you accept the moment without striving for a specific outcome.

How to begin:

Sit relaxed but alert, cross-legged on the floor or on a chair or couch with your feet flat on the ground. Keep your back straight and your hands resting on your lap or knees.

Close your eyes (optional) and bring your attention to the sensation of your breath as it moves in and out of your body. Feel the rise and fall of your chest or the air entering and leaving your nostrils. This serves as your anchor to the present moment.

Inevitably, your mind will wander to thoughts, feelings, or sensations. When this happens, notice it, acknowledge the thought (without judgment), and gently bring your focus back to the breath or another point of focus.

When thoughts, emotions, or physical sensations arise, observe them as if you are a witness. You can label them and then allow them to pass without engaging with them. For example, if a thought or emotion arises, you might label it gently "thinking," "feeling," or "worrying," and then let it pass without getting involved or reacting to it.

Whenever you notice your attention drifting away, gently return your focus to your breath or another anchor like the body. This practice of repeatedly returning your attention to the present is central to mindfulness meditation.

The time you spend is up to you, but generally, allow ten to fifteen minutes so you do not feel rushed. Over time, this will likely expand as the benefits of meditation reveal themselves.

A Final Word

Meditation is a practice that brings us into the moment, relaxes our mind and body, and prepares us for contemplation. As you practice, you will become comfortable with a method that fits you and can be used anytime or anywhere. I have practiced meditation while driving down the road, in the doctor's office, and at the grocery store. Mindfulness can become the norm rather than the exception.

Chapter 13

Contemplation: The Key to Manifesting

What we plant in the soil of contemplation, we shall reap in the harvest of action.

Meister Eckhart

Christians and adherents from other religious faiths have practiced contemplation for thousands of years. In the early days of the church, there was no bible, and most ordinary people could not read it, even if there was one. Contemplating spiritual truth and learning to listen in spirit was their only way to progress spiritually.

Christian monks, beginning in the second and third centuries, developed the practice of contemplating scripture and spiritual truths. Over time, Christian mystics such as St. Teresa of Avila (1515-1582) and St. John of the Cross (1542-1591) spoke of union with God through contemplation, often describing states of love, peace, and transcendence. Madam Guyon (1648-1717) of the French nobility eventually became a mystic and leader of the Quietism movement. She wrote extensively about contemplative prayer and inner spiritual experience.

Most Christians today do not practice inner contemplation or listening prayer, mainly because their leaders have not taught them to do so. However, more are increasingly adopting contemplative practices as the internet has made information more accessible over the last twenty-five years.

Listening to the intuitive knowing in spirit is crucial to contemplation. It is the beginning point, if you will. It is also the key to revealing your spiritual desires into the physical world.

In this chapter, we will examine how to listen to the intuitive knowing of the Spirit and respond to this communication in and during contemplation. We will also explore the steps in contemplation by applying the quantum concepts covered in part two of this book. I will give you a practical outline with illustrations to guide you. We will also look at combining meditation with contemplation and using I AM affirmations on your true identity to transition from one to the other.

The goal is to learn how to practically apply contemplative meditation based on the reality of how God's universe is created to function.

Steps in Contemplation

In part two of the book, we reviewed a process based on the realities of quantum physics and the teachings of scripture. We said that where you place your attention and focus will determine the outcomes in your life. What you have been given through spiritual intuition (vision) you can then imagine as already done. What you imagine as already done, you can feel gratitude for as though it already exists. What you feel gratitude for, you can verbally give thanks for as though you already have it. And what you verbally give thanks for, you can trust the Source of all life to fulfill in the appropriate time and way that is in your highest interest.

The first step in contemplation is learning to listen to the Spirit through spiritual intuition. This sets the stage for where you will place your attention and focus during contemplation.

Develop Your Spiritual Intuition

A woman's intuition serves her well. What does that mean? Women seem to have a sixth sense, an intuition, men do not have. They know when something does not seem right, something needs to be done right away, or maybe they feel something is not the truth. Spiritual intuition is very much like this, but more than this. It can be a feeling, a thought, or a desire. It can be about something you are considering, a decision, a situation that requires wisdom, or something communicated to you but will make more sense in time. It could come unexpectedly, and you were not even considering it. This is spiritual intuition, the work of the Spirit that is one with your spirit communicating timely guidance, knowledge, and wisdom as you need it (Luke 5:22; John 5:19, 6:63, 14:12-13; Acts 8:26, 29, 13:2, 3; Galatians 2:2, 5:16; I Corinthians 2:10-16; I John 2:27).

Spiritual intuition is the natural way for the believer and follower of Christ to live. It comes from within, the life that you are in union with and one with. It is based on love for oneself and others: "Love your neighbor as yourself." And "Do unto others as you would have them do unto you." Love is the power that leads us in spirit each moment if we have trained our soul to focus on our spirit and to listen.

This means transitioning from living based on external stimuli to living based on internal spiritual stimuli or intuition. For instance, one must grow more connected to one's feelings and thoughts to be more conscious of them and see one's thoughts as one with one's spirit rather than separate from one's spirit. The inner spirit, one with Christ's spirit, always leads, guides, and communicates through your feelings, desires, and thoughts. This may be difficult to understand, but it is the reality of our union with Christ.

Once we become more sensitive to and aware of the intuitive nature of the Spirit each moment, external things such as reading the Bible, listening to a sermon, watching a movie, reading the news, or even listening to a song become opportunities for spiritual communication on levels we have never experienced. Everything is spiritual, and nothing is to be seen as good or evil but rather an opportunity to listen, learn, and grow in connection with your spirit.

Developing the ability to sense your spiritual intuition is essential to living as a spiritual person. It cannot be taught but can be learned—not by reading books or acquiring more spiritual knowledge. The spiritual person learns to live by spiritual intuition one moment at a time, one experience at a time. It comes from within as the individual focuses on their spirit within. Where your focus goes, your energy flows, determining your outcomes.

The more you live with an inward focus, the greater your sensitivity to the inner voice of the Spirit and the awareness or intuition of what you need to know and do in each moment. You will live based on the reality of who you are: a spiritual being with a soul inhabiting a physical body. Spirit is who you are, the incredible energy that is unseen and powerful. Learn to live each moment by that power.

"But how?" you might ask. Listen, listen, listen. Go inward. "Be still and know I AM God." You are one with God. Go to your spirit in that oneness, be still, be in the moment, acknowledge your I AMness with God, your fantastic power as a spiritual being one with the Divine Life, and then listen. He will do the rest.

Develop Your Spiritual Visualization

We discussed the importance of visualizing the possibilities from a quantum perspective. This applies to your spiritual intuition. Spiritual intuition allows the Spirit to guide you into your desires and the will of God, which are the same thing when you are living from within. This spiritual guidance will reveal and develop a vision that applies to you and what you need to see for it to come about. This vision allows you to fully embrace the possibilities and eventually see from a greater perspective.

God does not give you a vision of everything at once, which would overwhelm your soul. Instead, he offers it in chunks that you can manage. One thing at a time when you need it. But it requires developing your spiritual intuition, listening, and responding to what you hear and see.

When I initially received the vision for Abiding in Agape, it was only focused on teaching the grace message of God's unconditional agape love. I had desired to teach this message for many years but did not have the opportunity to do it full-time, independent of other responsibilities. But things began to happen when I saw it in my spirit and embraced the vision from my spiritual intuition. Soon, I was invited to teach a small group. Over time, I received more from the Spirit to teach.

Eventually, several small group members encouraged me to take what I was teaching and put it into a book for broader dissemination. I had never authored a book and did not consider myself a writer. But I had something to write. The following year, I began to write what would eventually be my first book, *Alignment of Authentic Love: Living Your Highest Life*, which was published in 2023.

At each moment, the Spirit, through my intuition, has given me what I need to know and see to take the next step on this journey. I am learning to listen and see from my spirit and become comfortable living that way. The same is true for you. You can live moment by moment, with a vision of what you desire in spirit, and see it before it manifests physically.

Embrace it, respond to it, and experience life on a level you have never known before.

Develop Consistent Spiritual Communion

The Apostle Paul wrote, *"Pray without ceasing,"* in I Thessalonians 5:17. "No one can do that and live life—we must work, provide, and care for our families." Then why write it? Communicating with the Spirit each moment while fulfilling our responsibilities is possible. This is part of living from our spiritual intuition, in moment-by-moment communion with the Spirit. Living by our spirit, listening, and responding is possible at work, home, or other activities.

As we learn to listen and visualize in spirit, engaging with the Spirit continuously becomes natural. I will sometimes be at the store shopping, and the Spirit will speak to me in my spirit (not an audible voice). I will then respond, and a conversation will occur in spirit. I am never alone; no one is ever alone. The Spirit lives within you and desires to commune with you each moment.

I was coming home from the East Coast, where I had spent time with friends, flying standby using my youngest son's benefits with the airline he works for as a pilot. When you fly standby, you are not guaranteed a seat; you are positioned in line if a seat is available after all paying passengers are aboard. Having arrived at the airport in the morning, each flight was full, and I had to wait until the next flight to see if I would get on, usually several hours later. By 5:00 p.m., I began to wonder if I should reserve a room in a hotel and plan to try the next day.

The last flight out was at 7:00 p.m. My spiritual intuition had told me all day, "Do not get a hotel room or leave the airport; you will get on a flight." So, I stayed and envisioned myself on a plane, in a comfortable seat, arriving at my destination. I began to feel gratitude for it and thanked the Spirit that I was already home and enjoying time with my wife.

The last flight looked full, but there ended up being six open seats, and the fifth one went to me. Not only that, the seat was in an emergency exit row, which had much more legroom, and as someone who is 6'3, I always appreciate extra legroom! As I settled in for the three-hour flight, I thanked the Spirit for the encouragement to stay and not leave.

This is everyday living for the spiritual person if you are willing to develop consistent spiritual communion with the Spirit of all life within you. Anyone can do it; there are no remarkable or designated people. We are all equal. You can do this if you are willing to see that it is already yours and lives within you. This includes Christians and non-Christians, meaning everyone.

Practicing Contemplation

Part two of the book reviewed how the universe works at both quantum and macro levels. Understanding these concepts lets us apply them to contemplation and see how to do so deeply through our spiritual intuition.

What you contemplate must be something you desire Working on things you do not want will attract those things to you. Instead of focusing on things you do not want, think about what you do want and focus on it.

Focused Intention

Where you place your attention and then focus is the development of your intention.

Let us say you have placed your attention on your career. You intend to find a new job that will allow you to take the next steps in your career goals. You sense this is how you have been led through your spiritual intuition.

Focus on what you want, not what you do not want. Focused intention is about setting the stage for you to imagine it.

Using Your Imagination

Next, I want you to imagine yourself in what you visualize. As a spiritual being, you can access all the power in the universe to use your imagination; it lives within you. Close your eyes and imagine (see) yourself driving to your new job, as though you already have the job. Imagine parking your car, getting out, and entering the building. Imagine getting out of the elevator and walking to your new office as if you already have the job. In your imagination, you begin to manifest because you have a vision of what you desire and can now see yourself already having it and participating in it.

By picturing this, you bring it into the present tense as though it is already done. The universe has been created to respond to what you focus on with intention, vision, and imagination.

What would you like to do next in your career, and what level of leadership do you want? Detail the type of company, the people you want to work with, and the growth opportunities with that company. It is essential to be as specific as possible.

Leave the timing, company name, where, and other factors for the Spirit to determine. Your job is to be specific about the type of company and the job. For instance:

- My new job has supervisory responsibilities, allowing me to oversee staff and junior managers (assuming you have some experience in this area; beware of trying to avoid the necessary development in each stage of career growth). This job pays a minimum of XXX annually, and offers complete health, pension plan, and generous paid time off.
- The company has a domestic and international footprint and creates a positive work environment for its employees. My new job also allows exposure to top management and executives for career advancement.

- My boss appreciates my experience and skills and supports me in my career opportunities and growth. My new coworkers are also supportive and enjoy working with me, and vice versa.

Once you have this written down, shorten it into a workable statement. Notice I did not write "I want," "I hope," or "I wish." Never use those words! Always focus on the present tense, as though the job is yours.

Visualize What You Imagined

The next step is to visualize the job you have just focused on in detail. Close your eyes and visualize your business card title and your office's appearance. Visualize the office reception area, elevator, and conference rooms. This is your job now; can you see it?

You may say, "I don't know what the place will look like or my exact title." That does not matter to the Spirit (or universe, as all things are in the universal Christ). What matters is that you focus and can see what you desire fully. That is what you will attract. Quantum physics makes this clear.

It is best if you see everything you wrote down in detail. This means using your right brain versus your left brain. The left brain is the part that focuses on concrete material things, logic-oriented, and numbers-oriented. Your right brain is the home of your imagination and focuses on abstract, creative images, memories, and other things. Close your eyes and let your right brain take over. It may take some time, but keep practicing until you can visualize it. If you do not use your right brain often, you will need time to get comfortable with this practice.

For those who are more creative, this may be a little easier. Start slowly, try to see one thing, and then build on that. Be patient with yourself; you are developing a skill you will use for the rest of your life.

Feelings of Gratitude

Now that you can imagine yourself already having your desire as directed by your spiritual intuition, it is time to feel as though you already have it. In chapter seven, we saw the importance of feelings and raising our vibrations through gratitude. It is an essential part of realizing your desires. The higher the feelings of gratitude, as though you already have it, the more that feeling will attract what you desire. Remember, everything is energy, including thoughts and feelings. Quantum physics clarifies that the universe is constructed so that energy attracts like energy to itself. When you purposefully raise your feelings, you tell the universe you are ready for what you are focused on. It will, by its very nature, manifest that desire for you. It can be no other way.

Let us continue with the illustration of the job you want to manifest. Now that you have imagined yourself in that job, can you feel gratitude as though you already have it? Gratitude is a present-tense feeling by its very nature. If I feel grateful for the job, I must have the job already. Most of us want to wait until we have something to feel gratitude, but the universe was not constructed to work this way. Feel gratitude as though you already have it, and then it will, in time, show itself in physical form.

An excellent way to practice this is the same way you give thanks for the food you are about to eat. You do not wait to see the food before feeling grateful for it. That is not how faith works. We must first feel gratitude for what we desire before it appears. It is easy to be grateful for the food we already have, but it is much more difficult to feel gratitude when we have no food. Can you sit at your dinner table, close your eyes, see the job you intend to have and yourself doing it, and then feel gratitude as though it is already yours?

Do not wait for the feelings; you can produce gratitude, especially if you can imagine the job and see it as already yours.

Jesus was with His disciples, and a great crowd gathered to listen to Him teach. Towards the end of the day, Jesus asked Philip, one of His disciples, how they could feed all the people. Philip responded that a month's wages would not be enough to feed such a large crowd, with over five thousand men, not counting women and children. But there was a boy who had five barley loaves and two fish. Then Jesus did something interesting: He had the disciples tell the people to sit down, and then *He blessed the food* and had the disciples pass it out to the people.

When they were done eating, they gathered up what was left over, and there were twelve baskets full of scraps! Jesus did not wish that they had food or ask for food. He thanked God for the food and passed it out to them. To give thanks, you must first feel a sense of gratitude, which drives the willingness to give thanks. In other words, Jesus functioned like He had the food He needed. Philip reasoned with his ability and concluded that they could not do it. Jesus functioned as though He already had the food He needed and felt grateful for it, leading Him to give thanks.

That is how faith works because it is how the universe works.

Would you be willing to see the unseeable, feel gratitude for what is not in material form, and function as though you already have it? That is the key to thriving, not just surviving. See it, feel it, and function as if it is already done. Do not wait for the universe to send you what you want. Feel gratitude inside you and act like you already have what you want.

Giving Thanks Verbally

Verbal confession is the energy that releases feelings of gratitude. When you feel gratitude, the natural response is verbal thanksgiving. For instance, if I feel gratitude for the job I imagine myself currently having, I could say as an expression of thanks, "I am grateful for my new job in management." Use the present tense to express the gratitude and joy you feel at already having the job. This puts the vibe of gratitude and thanks into the atmosphere for the universe to respond to in time. Avoid "I wish," or "I hope," or "if it is Your will."

Those are excuses for not living in the moment with God. You might say, "I may not know if it is God's will." Did it come from your spiritual intuition or your ego? You know, and the Spirit will quickly show you if you ask. Worrying about things like that is unnecessary when we live by our spirit. Focus and give thanks that the job is already yours. When, where, and how is God's business. Seeing it as already yours is your business.

What we say has tremendous power and impacts the direction of our lives. Some clients I work with express negativity, doubt, and even condemnation towards themselves. "I'll never get that job, I know that." "Good things rarely happen to me." "I always get disappointed when I really want something." On and on. You just guaranteed it stays that way with your words! By saying these things, you are directing the universe God created not to send the job, potential spouse, new home, or good health, etc. As we said earlier, Jesus emphasized this:

> *Have faith in God. For assuredly, I say to you, whoever says to this mountain, 'Be removed and be cast into the sea,' and does not doubt in his heart, but believes that those things he says will be done, he will have whatever he says. Therefore I say to you, whatever things you ask when you pray, believe that you receive them, and you will have them.*
> Mark 11:22-24 NKJV

Verbal confession aligns your brain, body, and spirit and points them energetically in the same direction. You confidently declare to God's universe something as done even though you cannot see or touch it. "But what if it doesn't happen"? Again, the when, where, and how of something is none of your business. It may take days or years. If this is not God's will, then the Spirit will lead you into His will. This requires trust. We walk in the light that we have and let God worry about course corrections.

Abraham and Sara waited years for God to fulfill His promise of a child to them. In time, they lost hope, and Sara gave Abraham her handmaid, Hagar, to have a child in her stead. This was never God's plan, but God worked through their plan B and, in time, fulfilled plan A, when Issac arrived. Do we go outside plan A? Yes, but do not worry; God will fulfill Plan A in His time and way. Our part is to live each moment in gratitude and thanks that whatever we have put our focus and intention on is done.

Remember, faith is believing those things that are not as though they were because, with God, they are (Romans 4:17). Live your life as though you already have it with confidence and gratitude. This pathway of spiritual intuition and life leads one to thrive.

Release Control of the Outcomes

Now, the hard part is to release what you have focused on with intention, visualization, and imagining having it with gratitude and verbal thanks to God. Let go of it and give God the when, where, and how. He knows better than you do when, where, and how it should occur. All our attempts to control outcomes will eventually feed stress and anxiety. Attempts to control come from fear. We fear that we will not have what we want when we want it or think we need it, and the consequences that go with that are usually painful for us and those we love. But trust is more important than getting what we want.

Learning to trust occurs over time as we embrace the moment and accept it as a gift. This moment is precisely what is needed, and what was planned. There are no mistakes as we think of them, and experience is never wasted in God's economy. All of it is for our learning and our highest good.

Continuing the illustration of the job, once you have given thanks with feelings of gratitude, then letting go of the outcome releases the responsibility for when and how it manifests itself. This alleviates the need for anxiety or fear, as we are focused on the moment with gratitude, knowing it is done. You could say, "I am so grateful for my new job." Or, "I am thankful that God has been so trustworthy with my new job." Keep it in the present tense, with gratitude and thankfulness, but make it clear that the responsibility of manifesting it at the proper time rests with God and not you.

Does that mean you do not need to look for a job? Of course not. That is necessary for any job search and complements what you are doing with meditation and contemplation. The willingness to submit resumes proves that you are confident in what you have trusted God with. We are co-laborers with Christ, not spectators.

When I became ill with a neurological condition, it was very disruptive, difficult, and painful. I went to over twenty doctors of many specialties. But none of them could help me. My primary care doctor eventually told me he could not help me and that I did not need to see him again. I felt depressed and hopeless. My anxiety also increased because I knew I could not control the outcome.

One day, I realized that all my efforts were not getting me anywhere. So, I thanked God that He would either heal me or provide what I needed to deal with the pain and difficulty. From that point on, the outcome was no longer in my hands. I thanked Him for what I was learning and that He would lead me to what I needed to know and do so I could function.

One year later, a chiropractor recommended a nurse practitioner who focused on helping people with neurological conditions. I went to him, and he advised a procedure no doctor had pursued. This test came back positive and revealed that I was dealing with small nerve fiber neuropathy which was impacting my autonomic nervous system. Finally, an answer! This allowed the doctors to adjust my medication and for me to start practicing meditation to help manage my anxiety. Eventually, I learned more about contemplation and added that to my meditation practice.

Today, I live a very productive life, spiritual coaching and leadership coaching, writing and hosting podcasts on the Grace Awakening Network, gantv.com, and well-known podcast apps. And sharing messages and interacting on social media platforms. This would not have been possible had I not released the responsibility for the outcome to the Spirit of all life.

Meditation and Contemplation Together

We want to combine everything in a workable process that you can use anytime, anywhere. Meditation leads to being present now, the I AM. Contemplation is being in the moment and focusing on that which spiritual intuition, in oneness with Christ, has revealed. Combining these will give you the foundation to manifest the life you want in your union with the Divine Life.

Begin with the meditation style you are most comfortable with to bring you into the moment. Once you are entirely in the moment, begin to transition to I AM affirmations that you would like to focus on: "I AM enough, I AM loved, I AM valued, I AM powerful." Slowly use the I AM affirmations to deepen your focus on the moment and your true self in spirit.

Now, you can transition to contemplation focused on what the Spirit has revealed, and your desires. The important thing is to allow your mind to visualize what you desire and then imagine yourself already having what you focus on and actively enjoying it while increasing your feelings of gratitude, thankfulness, and joy.

Below is an example of a worksheet I use to quantify what I initially contemplated. In time, I did not need the worksheet, but had it memorized to use as I liked. So will you.

Contemplation Worksheet

Focus:	My focus is on the next step in my career.
Intention:	My purpose is to seek the next step in my career that is in line with my purpose and inner spiritual direction.
Imagine:	Everything is possible for me, nothing is too great or difficult. My mind is open to imagine all the possibilities that are mine this moment in the Divine Life.
Visualize:	My new job has an open office environment with high ceilings, plenty of space and windows with great views.
Gratitude:	I feel grateful for my new job and all it offers.
Thankfulness:	I am thankful for my new job and all that it provides me.
Release:	I release this to the Spirit for physical manifestation in the appropriate way and time.

This worksheet is something I use when the Spirit reveals something to me. In my journal, I contemplate many such items. Not every day. There are too many of them. But several each day. Some have manifested, others are in the process of manifesting, and others have not. That is the nature of the universe God created. Our part is not to dictate how, when, or even to what extent. Ours is to be faithful and imagine it as though it has already been done, with deep gratitude and thankfulness, speaking that thankfulness out loud. Then, release it to the Spirit and let the Spirit do the rest.

Let life flow to you in spirit. Your part is to respond and be in the moment. You are a full contributor but not a controller. If something needs to be adjusted, the Spirit will clarify it. If you are not on the right track, the Spirit will clarify through your intuition. Focus on the moment and what has been revealed, and leave the rest to the Divine Life.

This meditation and contemplation will become much easier, and you will not need to follow a worksheet. You will know by heart what is needed, like an inner tool for inner work. However, new skills must be learned and mastered initially. There are no free lunches, as they say. Use my example worksheet initially when organizing your thoughts and desires. Remember to keep everything in the present tense, not "I want, will, wish, or hope." Function as if it is done because, with God, it is done.

A Final Word

A warning: This is not a magical formula but a spiritual way of living and seeing the world. It is a response to the world God created based on how Jesus lived His life and how we are to live our lives.

If you want an easy life, this is not for you. I cannot promise you that. If you want to be rich, this is not for you. If you want someone to fall in love with you or love you, I cannot promise that. Those things are in God's hands and are secondary to what is essential: love working through faith.

Love is the focus because God is love (1 John 4:16). When we manifest new jobs, money, companies, or opportunities, we open the door to loving people in more ways than if we did not.

Love is the most significant manifestation of who we are in Christ.

I have come that they may have life, and that they may have it more abundantly.
John 10:10b NKJV

> *I have come as a light to shine in this dark world, so that all who put their trust in me will no longer remain in the dark.*
> John 12:46 NLT

> *I tell you the truth, the Son can do nothing by himself. He does only what he sees the Father doing. Whatever the Father does, the Son also does. For the Father loves the Son and shows him everything he is doing. In fact, the Father will show him how to do even greater works than healing this man. Then you will truly be astonished.*
> John 5:19, 20 NLT

Jesus said he came into the world so people would have life *(Zoe)* and have it abundantly, or you could translate it as "superabundantly." How? To be a light in a world where people's minds have been darkened by the lies they believe about themselves, God, and others. Jesus came so we would no longer live in those lies, in darkness. Trusting in Him means trusting what He says by seeing how He lives and works. How did Jesus do the work? By doing only what He saw His Father do. He did so because He knew the Father loved Him and was willing to show Him the work God wanted Him to do. This is a life that thrives, not just survives.

Do you see it? Jesus did not try to earn money or own things. He sought the welfare of those around Him. He wanted them to have abundant lives, living in the truth of who they are in the Divine Life. He did this from an inner communion with His Father in spirit. The Father then showed Jesus everything He was to do.

Just as Jesus lived this way, we are to live that way. Our lives should bless and seek the good of those around us. We love by seeking the highest good of our neighbor, the person whom God brings our way each day. Love is the focal point. When we live from the inner life of our spirit, the Spirit will show us what to do, where to go, who to talk to, and when to do it. We will intuitively know this each moment in spirit. A new job becomes an opportunity to love other people. When we manifest that job, it is love in action. And with that, there is immense joy and contentment. That is the life that thrives with purpose, harmony, and power from within. It is the life you were made to live each day.

Conclusion

If you want to find the secrets of the universe, think in terms of energy, frequency, and vibration.

Nikola Tesla

Every intention sets energy into motion, whether you are aware of it or not.

Gary Zukav

We can unknowingly experience what psychologists call the Dunning-Kruger effect in the journey of inward spiritual maturity and growth, which includes meditation and contemplation. The Dunning-Kruger effect describes how people often overestimate their abilities in the early stages of learning something new because they do not know enough to recognize the depth of what they do not fully understand.

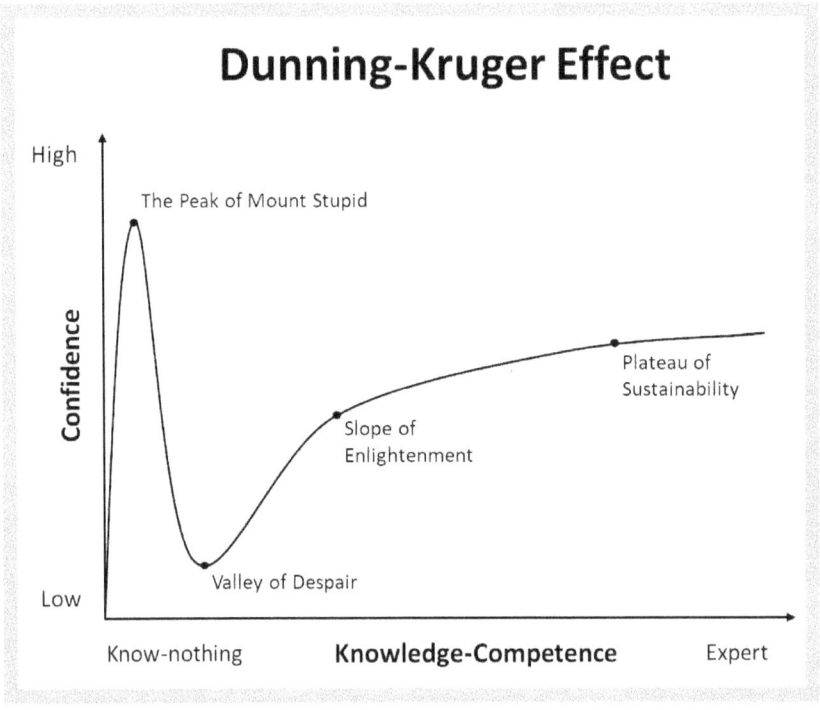

Figure 14.1 Dunning-Kruger Effect Graph. **The beginning point for failure is The Peak of Mount Stupid when people are highly confident but do not realize how little they know. Eventually, they find themselves in the Valley of Despair, feeling overwhelmed at how little they know. In time, this can lead to greater enlightenment, growth, and becoming competent and knowledgeable practitioners of a skill.**

Beginners in meditation and contemplation, with only a surface-level experience of calm and clarity, may feel as though they have already mastered the practice. They assume it is simply sitting still and quieting the mind, unaware that true meditation involves much more —facing inner turbulence, cultivating sustained attention, and developing a nuanced awareness of one's thoughts and emotions. This initial overconfidence can create a false sense of progress, leading beginners to believe that meaningful results will come quickly and easily.

However, as they continue, they soon realize that meditation is not as straightforward as it seems. The mind, which initially appeared so easy to calm, begins to resist. Thoughts race, emotions rise, and long practice periods yield little of the initial peace they felt. This is the point where many recognize the gap between their early confidence and the actual skill required.

The Dunning-Kruger effect reminds us that meaningful spiritual growth in inward meditation and contemplation requires moving beyond the early illusion of mastery, enduring the difficult phases of self-doubt, and eventually embracing the lifelong nature of the inward, contemplative practice.

Imagine someone who, in the early days of their practice, feels an overwhelming sense of accomplishment. They sit quietly, focus on their breath, and soon notice how calm they feel afterward. "This isn't so hard," they think, convinced they have grasped the essence of meditation in just a few sessions. At this stage, confidence soars, but it is built on a shallow foundation. Like a novice hiker standing at the base of a mountain, they may admire the landscape and assume the summit is just a short climb away, unaware of the vast, hidden terrain ahead.

As weeks turn into months, this beginner starts to encounter unexpected challenges. Their mind will not stay still, emotions they did not anticipate begin to surface, and the calm they initially found so quickly seems elusive. This is when reality hits—the journey is far more complex than they first imagined. Confidence begins to waver, replaced by doubt. The hiker who once marveled at the ease of the trail now finds themselves in the thick of a dense forest, realizing the mountain is much taller than it seemed. This is where they either quit or, with renewed humility, press on.

Those who persevere gradually develop a deeper understanding. Over time, they stop chasing quick results and begin to appreciate the subtlety of meditation and contemplation. They realize that it is not about conquering the mind but about sitting with its restlessness and learning from it. Confidence returns, not in the form of arrogance, but as a quiet, balanced knowing that progress is a lifelong process. They have climbed high enough to glimpse how far they have come, yet they also see no final summit—only continuous exploration.

This progression mirrors the classic path described by the Dunning-Kruger effect: the initial overconfidence of beginners, the humbling dip in self-assurance as they become aware of their limitations, and, finally, the stable competence of experienced practitioners who have learned through time, patience, and self-reflection. How long this journey takes varies significantly from person to person. It may be a matter of months before they hit the inevitable dip in confidence. For others, it could take years of consistent practice to reach a point where they feel grounded in their meditation and contemplation. But those who stay the course, like seasoned hikers who learn to navigate the landscape without rushing, eventually find that mastery is not the goal—the ongoing process of walking the path daily is what genuinely matters.

Be Patient with Yourself

You have heard the adage that life is a marathon, not a race. This is never truer than in our inward spiritual journey. We have covered a lot of material in a limited number of pages. It is highly unlikely you heard the message of this book in church, especially regarding quantum physics, God's general revelation, and spirituality. This means it is new to you and will take time to incorporate and become comfortable with it. Be patient with yourself; this is not a race. It is a marathon played out moment by moment.

Learn to be good to yourself by embracing the times when you struggle or feel stuck. These come because your ego is resisting change, taking you away from focusing on external stimuli and the rewards that go with them. Everything resists this change: from the world we live in to our family, friends, coworkers, and especially religious people. Therefore, to struggle as you learn and grow in this inward way is normal and to be expected. Lean into the struggle by being grateful for it and giving thanks.

For instance, "I am grateful that growing in the inward way of meditation and contemplation is a learning process, and I am making progress even when I cannot see it." Beating yourself up will accomplish nothing. However, positive affirmation can help when things are difficult.

Did you learn to ride a bike in a day? No, but the training wheels helped, and then, after the training wheels, came the inevitable falls that go with being a new rider. Failure is the process that leads you to more success. Avoid judging anything: it is a waste of your time.

The same can be said of driving a car. Initially, you start on the backstreets, parking lots, and away from other cars (hopefully). But, in time, you start driving on the streets and highways. Eventually, there is the first ticket and a fender bender. Failure is the price of eventual success; it comes with learning to be a competent driver. Do you stop driving altogether and pronounce yourself a failure because of these things? No, you return to the car, learn from your mistakes, and continue (unless you want to walk everywhere you go).

Pace yourself, love who you are, and embrace the moment. This journey of the inward way in meditation and contemplation will become the adventure of a lifetime. Loving yourself, being patient, and being good to yourself will assist you in that adventure.

You are right where you need to be, on time and on target. Nothing is wasted. Everything is working in God's economy for your growth and maturity.

Everything Is Energy Including You

It is easy to believe this life is the big R Reality when it is not. Reality is unseen; in the 95 percent you cannot see. At the most fundamental level, reality is unseen energy. Even for material things, such as yourself, reality is energy. You are living in a body having a human experience. But that body is made of energy, just as your soul and spirit are energy. Everything is energy, no matter what it is. Everything is in vibration, and this vibration has a level of frequency at which it vibrates. This fact can expand your world with unlimited possibilities, or it can be something you ignore or fail to appreciate from a spiritual perspective.

If embraced, it will impact how you see the world, people, and even the scriptures. The world will become a place of possibilities that have yet to be seen physically. People can be appreciated for their inherent value and connectedness to everything, including you. No longer "us" and "them," but "we."

With this understanding of general revelation, the scriptures can open in ways you have not seen before. Living by the Spirit can now be understood through the lens of unseen energy. You can begin to see yourself as an energy-being who is powerful and connected to the Divine Life (who IS the energy source), with all the possibilities that go with that. No more distance between you and God, but the reality of union and oneness together in this unified field.

Suppose you are willing to embrace God's general revelation, as in quantum physics. In that case, the Spirit can reveal other areas of general revelation that will open you to higher levels of consciousness you have never experienced.

Your understanding of special revelation, as seen in the scriptures, will be enhanced and benefit you and others. It is the pathway to living from within so you can thrive, not just survive.

Manifesting Love Is the Point

What is more significant than unconditional love? My years on this planet have taught me that nothing is more significant than unconditional love. Nothing.

The lyrics of the song "Love Is the Answer," sung by England Dan and John Ford Coley, make the point that the artist has tried everything and keeps coming back to the same answer: love. It is all about love. Manifesting that love is the point, always has been, always will be, even when we do not realize it. There is no greater calling, purpose, or plan than love.

I can remember the first time I heard that song. It was in 1980, after I had dropped my then-girlfriend off at her house. I was on my way home, and it came on the radio. That song grabbed me and has never let go after all these years. I knew at seventeen, entirely taught in the evangelical faith, that the song's message was truth—more truth than most of what I had learned in the church. Those two rock stars were more right in the simplest way than the many pastors and teachers I had listened to for all those years.

Why did I not change then and make that the focal point of my life? The same reason most people do not: ego. My ego (religious ego, in my case) would not allow it. I had to go through many life experiences and failures to come to the answer presented so clearly at seventeen.

It would take nearly forty years to do that. But that was what my ego needed. And the Spirit of all life was okay with that. A journey is just that, a journey, not a race. And coming to this conclusion for each person takes time.

Have you come to this conclusion yet? I hope you will. When you do, it will change everything.

The point is that love will show itself throughout your life. That is the reason I authored this book. You manifest the new job so you can love people at that job and care for your loved ones. The health you manifest is so you can love your family, the neighbors, those at your church and in your community. The finances you manifest are so you can love through paying your bills, caring for those in need, and giving to the things you are enthusiastic about.

When seen through the eyes of love, everything changes, and manifesting in the 5 percent becomes a privilege and, in some ways, a duty to those we live with.

Unfortunately, the church has not taught this spiritual reality over the years. I hope this book will fill that gap and allow you to live as the powerful spiritual being you already are in Christ and express that life outwardly through what you manifest.

Fulfill your purpose based on your passion and manifest through the Spirit with whom you are one, and in so doing, bless as many people (eternal energy-beings like yourself) as possible. What could be more important?

Five-Dimesional Living

I want to conclude by summarizing what I hope will be a journey for you into more profound experiences as a powerful spiritual being. I pray that you will live in that deeper state continually and enjoy the inheritance that is yours in Christ Jesus.

Our world has three dimensions: height, width, and length. These dimensions describe the physical space we experience daily, forming a three-dimensional (3D) environment.

CONCLUSION

However, there is also a five-dimensional reality: the physical, psychological, spiritual, conscious spiritual awareness, and active spiritual consciousness. The diagram in Figure 14.2 helps to illustrate this.

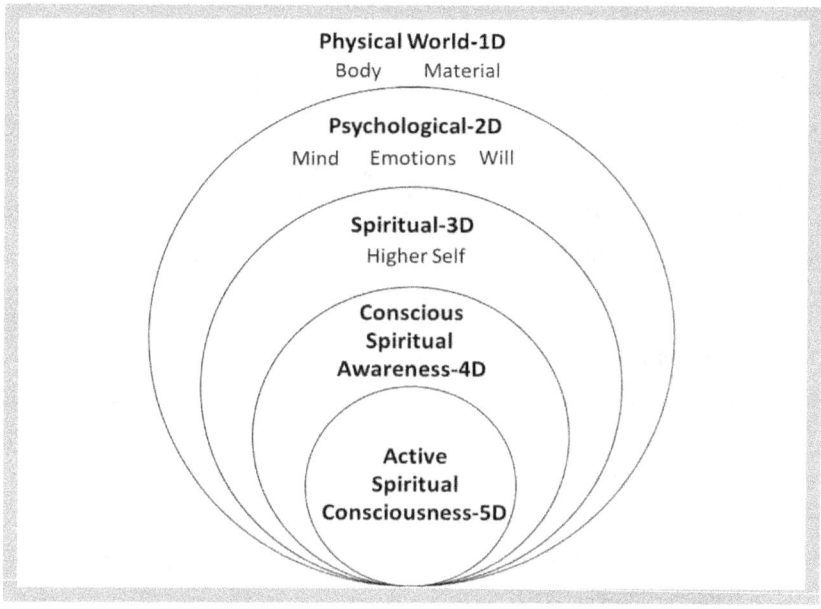

Figure 14.2 Five-Dimensional Living Diagram

The physical world-1D (first dimension) represents everything we can see, touch, smell, taste, and hear—anything related to the material world, most of which is outside us. Most people focus on this dimension and are rarely aware of the other dimensions. A few may discover the second dimension and its impact, but most are only aware of the first dimension. Because of this, they constantly pursue things in the physical world as though they are the primary reality. However, as we have seen, they are not. This leads to incredible frustration and a sense of emptiness that grows as we become 1D-focused.

Psychological-2D (second dimension) represents the soul with the mind, emotions, and will. This is the dimension of thinking, feeling, and actions. However, few people are aware of what they are thinking, feeling, or doing at any moment (though women tend to be aware of this dimension more than men). This dimension is challenging due to past traumas, hurts, and disappointments that have not healed. The emotional wounds from these things create a barrier to the spiritual dimension and develop false identities that, unknown to the individual, direct much of the decisions in the person's life. If an individual heals from the traumas, hurts and disappointments in the second dimension, then the third dimension becomes accessible, with the corresponding benefits of living from their spirit.

The Spiritual-3D (third dimension) is the reality of who you are as a spiritual being. Nothing is more accurate about who you are than the third dimension. This is your higher self or true self. You are a spirit; you have a soul that is learning and maturing, and you are doing so in a human body, having a human experience. You are a powerful spiritual being, one with the Divine Life. All that is true of Christ in your union with Him is true of you. Though, as we have said, you are you, and Christ is Christ. This is a mystery, but it is true. The traumas, hurts, and disappointments that have created emotional wounds in the soul ego have blocked your higher self in spirit. The false identities that result from these wounds have kept the Spirit from expressing itself freely in harmony with the soul. This is the goal: that you may be who you already are in spirit and express your true higher self through your soul and body in this alignment of authentic love. Few people are fully aware of their spirit, and even fewer focus on it. This is the source of most problems in the church and the world. Can you imagine the difference it would make if every person could focus on their spirit in complete alignment with their soul and body?

The spiritual dimension has two deeper levels that one can experience each moment. The first is what I call Conscious Spiritual Awareness-4D. This fourth dimension is when an individual is not only aware of the spiritual dimension but actively attempts to live in that dimension. Many Christians and unbelievers readily admit to spiritual realities and may speak of them occasionally. But that is as far as they go. A few make their spiritual higher self the focus of their soul. These begin to go deeper into this 4D and experience how it works, hone their skills to participate in it, and are willing to practice these skills even when it seems they are making no progress. They are conscious of the reality of their higher self and spirituality, but it is work for them. This is true of any new thing in our lives. It requires a time of trial and error to grow in our knowledge and skill level, as we saw in the Dunning-Kruger Effect Graph.

And we should not grow weary in well doing, for in due time, not fainting, we will reap a harvest.
Galatians 6:9 (My translation of the Greek.)

"Do not grow weary in well doing;" that is, in bringing your focus to this inner way of spirit. In time, it will pay off and your soul and others will be better for it. It takes time to live by the intuitive direction of the Spirit, to hear in the Spirit, and to learn to respond. Our minds are still not trained to focus, and neither are our emotions. We have lived an outer-focused life; this transition in the fourth dimension is the normal progression for growth and maturity in our skills and ability to see and hear spiritually.

The last is Active Spiritual Consciousness-5D. Here, we begin to live more naturally by our higher self. We are, to some degree, unconscious of doing it. Listening to the intuitive direction of the Spirit has become the norm, and gaining insights and knowledge from the Spirit has become our default setting. The fifth dimension of living is what we were created to be and do. Jesus lived a 5D life continuously, yet even

He had to mature and grow, being as human as we are. This is where we become unconsciously competent. We are now living in the flow of the spiritual river. Life is coming to us rather than us chasing it. Each moment is as it should be, and we do not fight it. We intuitively know what to do, and things come to us rather than through our effort and work. We are what we used to seek, not because we worked for it or earned it, but because we now see that in Christ, we were always what we were seeking. There is no longer good and evil, us and them, Satan vs. God, or the church vs. the world. There is simply union, oneness, love, peace, and the moment. God is, not because of faith, but because we know He is. And that knowing is grounded in love. Faith becomes a secondary matter. As Paul wrote,

Three things will last forever—faith, hope, and love—and the greatest of these is love.
I Corinthians 13:13 NLT

This is the inheritance of each person, no matter who they are, as all things are in the Divine Life. I hope and pray that as you grow in maturity and skill, you will increasingly enjoy a 5D life with all the benefits and blessings that go with it—not just for yourself but for all the energy-beings you encounter each day.

You Were Made to Thrive, Not Just Survive

You were made to thrive, not just survive! Do you believe that? I hope you do. This life is not for the special few who seem to have their act together, or God's chosen ones; it is for every person on this planet. The focus you put on your higher self will determine if you thrive or not. You can live in the power and movement of the river of the Spirit. Or you can swim upstream, working and striving to make things happen, trying to achieve and become. You can rest in Christ, knowing everything is done, focus inwardly on your spirit, and find everything you need there. Life will manifest for you rather than you working for it. Relationships, finances, career, family, friends, and the future are no longer your focus. You know now that living in the moment is what matters above all. This is a life that thrives.

Above all, are you willing to love yourself? I am convinced that until we do, we will struggle with an outer focus. Because there will always be something outside us that we think will help us become, achieve, or have. But none of that works. Embracing and loving yourself leads to an inner focus. You can rest in your soul because you are at peace with yourself. And when you love yourself just as you are, you will experience inner peace. That opens the door to manifesting in the 5 percent to love others. And loving yourself and others is what it means to love God.

May you thrive in the experience of love and grace as the powerful, complete spiritual being you are.

Appendix One: Meditation Practices

Meditation Practice #1

Sit in a quiet place with your eyes closed.
Begin to breathe in through your nose, hold the breath for several seconds, then breathe out through your mouth.
Focus on your breath as you inhale, then as you exhale.
As you breathe, breathe in from your belly rather than your upper body. Let the belly come out as you breathe in.
Now, as you continue to breathe, notice your head and the space your head takes up in the space you are in.
Now, notice your neck, the space your neck takes up in the space you are in.
Working your way down the body, notice your shoulders and the space they take up.
Notice your waist and the space your waist takes up.
Can you notice your hips and the space your hips take up?
Notice your upper legs and the space your upper legs take up.
Can you notice your knees and the space your knees take?
Notice your calves and the space your calves take up in space.

Notice your feet and the space your feet take up in space.
Now, can you notice your entire body and the space your entire body takes up in the space you are in?
As you continue breathing, with your eyes closed, begin to say some affirmations.
I AM Peace
I AM Loved
I AM Valued
I AM Accepted
I AM Enough
I AM Abundant
I AM Wonderful
I AM Grateful
As you say each affirmation, take a few seconds to think about it. What does it mean to you this moment to know you ARE peace? How does that bring inner peace to your soul?
And so on.
When you are done, give thanks for this meditation time.
Slowly open your eyes and notice the quietness of your heart and mind. As you go, enjoy this inner rest and peace.

Meditation Practice #2

Sit in a quiet place with your eyes closed.
Begin to breathe in through your nose, hold the breath for several seconds, then breathe out through your mouth.
Focus on your breath as you inhale, then as you exhale.
As you breathe, breathe in from your belly rather than your upper body. Let the belly come out as you breathe in.
Now, focus on the image of a waterfall or a beautiful meadow, or it could be a beach sunset. Ask yourself:
What do I see?
What colors do I see?
What do I hear?

What do I smell?
Is there a breeze?
Am I sitting or standing?
Is anyone with me?
How do I feel?
Be in the moment with that image, enjoying it thoroughly. Let it fully encompass your mind and emotions.
Now, in gratitude, give thanks for your time enjoying the beauty of that image.
Sit for a moment with your emotions of gratitude.
Take one affirmation and begin to say it to yourself.
I AM Enough.
I
AM
Enough
I AM Enough every moment.
Now, opening your eyes, slowly express thanks for this time of meditation and all you have received.

Appendix Two: Contemplation Instructions and Template

Use the template below to create your first contemplation practice. What has the Spirit shown you through your meditation?

What do you want to focus on and eventually manifest based on spirit revelation?

Are you ready to put it down on paper and begin to focus on it?

Focus: What will you focus on? Make it as specific and straightforward as possible.
Intention: What do you want to manifest? What is your intention in this contemplation practice? Shorter is better than longer.
Imagine: Now, can you let your imagination work for you to see the possibilities? Nothing is too great or too outside the box. Free your imagination to see as clearly as possible that which you desire.
Visualization: Can you visualize what you imagined? Can you see it in detail? Close your eyes and see it in your mind. Write it out in sentence form here so you can see it in your mind's eye each day during this exercise.

Gratitude: I feel grateful that _____. (Always present tense.)

Thankfulness: I AM thankful that _____. (Always present tense.)

Release: Trust the Spirit and your higher self to manifest this God-given desire at the proper time! But write it out so you can say it.

Contemplation Template

Focus:
Intention:
Imagine:
Visualization:
Gratitude:
Thankfulness:
Release:

Appendix Three: Affirmations

I AM Affirmations

I AM accepted
I AM abundant
I AM adored
I AM agape love
I AM blessed
I AM complete
I AM more than a conqueror
I AM a co-heir
I AM a co-creator
I AM excellent
I AM faithful
I AM forgiven
I AM gentle
I AM patience
I AM peace
I AM seated with Christ

I AM self-control
I AM strong
I AM sufficient
I AM righteousness
I AM transcendent
I AM valuable
I AM victorious
I AM whole
I AM wisdom
I AM wonderful
I AM giving
I AM good
I AM healed
I AM included
I AM joy
I AM kind
I AM life
I AM light
I AM loved
I AM the mind of Christ
I AM miraculous
I AM noble
I AM one Spirit with Christ

I AM Statements[1]

I AM more loving and forgiving every day.
I AM worthy of everything good in life.
I AM now a reflection of my highest self.
I AM a magnet for abundance and blessings in all forms.
I AM doing the best I can.
I AM a beautiful person inside and out.
I AM open to letting love flow into my experience now.

I AM tending to my desires and needs with love and compassion.
I AM loving myself more and more every day.
I AM getting to know myself on deeper levels.
I AM now seeing myself in a new, loving light.
I AM open to seeing myself in new ways that serve my highest good.
I AM worthy of connections that are loving, genuine and nourishing.
I AM ever evolving and ever-expanding.
I AM finding comfort in my own skin.
I AM free to learn and grow at my own pace.
I AM allowed to express myself.
I AM fine just the way I am.
I AM at peace with my past.
I AM surrounded by love.
I AM inhaling who I am, exhaling who I am not.
I AM my own best friend.
I AM giving myself the love I've always needed.
I AM taking my needs seriously and not feeling guilty about it.
I AM always in the right place at the right time.
I AM constantly being offered new opportunities for success.
I AM grateful for another day to make a positive contribution.
I AM a money magnet and attract money easily.
I AM becoming more and more successful every day.
I AM grateful for all the new opportunities that come my way.
I AM grateful for today's opportunities.
I AM ever expanding my belief of what's possible.
I AM now attracting the perfect career for my talents.
I AM flooded with opportunities every day.
I AM influential and respected in my field.
I AM in alignment with my soul's purpose.
I AM allowing joy to guide me.
I AM ready for what is to come.
I AM living in total abundance.
I AM so grateful that my wildest dreams are coming true.

I AM so grateful that Christ is always working for my greater good.
I AM excited to know that things are always working out for me.
I AM blessed beyond measure.
I AM daring to be different and being rewarded for it.
I AM grateful that my success has no limits.
I AM aligned with the energy of abundance.
I AM open and ready to receive miracles.
I AM getting stronger and healthier every day.
I AM allowing my body to heal.
I AM allowing well-being to flow to me now.
I AM letting go of all resistance.
I AM allowing my cells to replenish and re-calibrate.
I AM forgiving and releasing all that hurts me.
I AM willing to listen to what my body is telling me.
I AM releasing worrisome thoughts that do not serve me.
I AM calling in light and love to replenish my cells.
I AM forgiving all those who have hurt me.
I AM forgiving and letting go of my mistakes.
I AM releasing the resentment that hurts me.
I AM releasing irritations that are trapped in my body.
I AM trusting the journey.
I AM worthy of healing.
I AM a timeless, eternal being connected to the wisdom of the universe.
I AM healing little by little, and there is no rush.
I AM energetic and grateful for my life.
I AM relaxed, centered, and refreshed in my present state of mind.
I AM grateful for this beautiful, healthy body that I have.
I AM grateful that my body is capable of healing on its own.
I AM now lovingly releasing all blockages that had manifested in my body.
I AM grateful for my body and every amazing thing it can do.
I AM appreciating my body and all the pleasure it brings me.

I AM aware that my body knows exactly what to do in order to heal itself.
I AM observing my emotions without getting attached to them.
I AM nourishing my body with food that makes it feel good.
I AM feeling better and better every day.
I AM enjoying moving my body in ways that feel good.
I AM sending love and light to every organ in my body.

Notes

Preface

1. Rene Girard, *The Girard Reader* (New York: The Crossroad Publishing Company, 1996), 9.
2. Ibid., 69.

Introduction

1. Hartmut Neven, "Meet Williow, Our State-Of-The-Art Quantum Chip," Blog.Google.com, December 9, 2024. https://blog.google/technology/research/google-willow-quantum-chip/.

1. Deconstructing Beliefs that Hold You Back

1. Gina Zurlo, Todd Johnson, Peter Crossing, "World Christianity and Religions 2022: A Complicated Relationship," *International Bulletin of Mission Research* Vol. 46 no.1 (2022):71–80. https://www.researchgate.net/publication/357271199_World_Christianity_and_Religions_2022_A_Complicated_Relationship.
2. Todd Johnson, "Christianity is Fragmented – Why?", GordonConwell.edu, November 6, 2019. https://www.gordonconwell.edu/blog/christianity-is-fragmented-why/.
3. I John 2:27.

2. Changing Your Perspective

1. The term "dogma" generally refers to a principle or set of principles that are believed to be incontrovertibly true or binding without any need for proof or justification. In a religious context, dogma often refers to doctrines or beliefs considered essential to the faith and not subject to debate or revision. In a broader sense, dogma can also refer to any strongly held belief or ideology that is treated as absolute truth. The word dogma is often used in a derogatory sense to refer to beliefs that are seen as rigid, dogmatic, or inflexible and which may be imposed on others without regard for their individual beliefs or opinions. This is true of Christianity in general. Believe what we tell you and stop asking questions.
2. "Planck Mission Brings Universe Into Sharp Focus." Nasa.Gov. NASA, March 21, 2013. https://www.jpl.nasa.gov/news/planck-mission-brings-universe-into-sharp-focus/

3. Robert Krulwich, "Which Is Greater, The Number Of Sand Grains On Earth Or Stars In The Sky?" NPR.Org. Accessed March 27, 2025. https://www.npr.org/sections/krulwich/2012/09/17/161096233/which-is-greater-the-number-of-sand-grains-on-earth-or-stars-in-the-sky.
4. "Einstein's Equation: E = Mc2." Atomicarchive.Com. Accessed May 28, 2023. https://www.atomicarchive.com/science/physics/einsteins-equation.html.
Einstein's formula is $E=MC^2$, with E standing for energy, M standing for mass (matter), and C^2 standing for the speed of light squared. At its most basic, the formula means energy = matter. This is then multiplied by the speed of light squared (a very big number). Because C^2 is such a large number, a very small amount of mass can produce much energy.
5. For a brief history of humankind written for non-scholars, see Yuval Noah Harari's book, "Sapiens, A Brief History of Humankind," Harper Perennial, 2018.
6. Guthrie, S. E.. "anthropomorphism." Encyclopedia Britannica, April 15, 2008. https://www.britannica.com/topic/anthropomorphism.
7. When I say love without expectations, many people accuse me of hyper-grace or encouraging people just to do whatever they want. As if enjoying this Divine love and grace will result in the destruction of a person's physical and emotional life. Nothing could be further from the truth. People are already doing whatever they want under the current evangelical legalistic model. Legalism inevitably leads to more destructive behavior. Usually, people hide it, so others won't find out. If you are a pastor or elder, don't deceive yourself into believing that people are adhering to the moral and ethical standards you have laid out for them, or the threats of hell and punishment in the afterlife. If there is anything I have learned over the last thirty years of spiritual coaching and ministering to people, it is that preaching the law actually increases the behavior to violate it. Only grace through agape changes the inner heart and releases people to see and be who they already are in Christ. Love and grace, not rules and standards, keep a person grounded. Failure is how we learn; it is the contrast between our self-indulgence and its failures to fulfill us that creates the opportunity to live in grace through love as a spiritual person. Laws and rules do the same thing. Inevitably, the person will fail, and it is through failure that they can begin to live from their inner spirit rather than trying to be "holy."

3. A Quantum Leap

1. "Mass & Energy: One And The Same." The Institution for Science Advancement, July 12, 2019. http://ifsa.my/articles/mass-energy-one-and-the-same.
2. Sharp, Tim, and Djordjevic, Daisy. "What Is an Atom? Facts about the Building Blocks of the Universe." Live Science, December 15, 2021. https://www.livescience.com/37206-atom-definition.html.
3. "States of Matter." Purdue University. Chemistry Department of Purdue University, Accessed June 21, 2023. https://www.chem.purdue.edu/gchelp/atoms/states.html#:~:text=gas%20vibrate%20and%20move%20freely,move%20from%20place%20to%20place.

4. Stanborough, Rebecca J. "What Is Vibrational Energy?" Healthline. November 13, 2020. (Updated 23 September 2024). https://www.healthline.com/health/vibrational-energy. The research in this area continues on whether vibrations from many different levels physiologically and psychologically contribute to personal health, motivation, and goal achievement.
5. Di Biase, Francisco. "Quantum Entanglement of Consciousness and Space-Time A Unified Field of Consciousness." NeuroQuantology 17, no. 03 (2019): 80-84. Accessed June 26, 2023. https://www.researchgate.net/profile/Francisco-Di-Biase/publication/332857426_Quantum_Entanglement_of_Consciousness_and_Space-Time_A_Unified_Field_of_Consciousness/links/5d85460c299bf1996f82f9f1/Quantum-Entanglement-of-Consciousness-and-Space-Time-A-Unified-Field-of-Consciousness.pdf.
6. Bruce Rosenblum, Fred Kuttner, *Quantum Enigma: Physics Encounters Consciousness* (New York: Oxford University Press, 2011), 188.
7. Brian Clegg, *Dark Matter and Dark Energy: The Hidden 95% of the Universe* (London: Icon Books Ltd., 2019), 10.

4. Consciousness and Possibilities

1. Goswami, Amit, *God Is Not Dead: What Quantum Physics Tells Us About Our Origins And How We Should Live* (Charlottesville: Hampton Roads Publishing Company, Inc., 2012) 24.
2. Hamer, Ashley. "The Double-Slit Experiment Cracked Reality Wide Open." Discovery.com. August 1, 2019. https://www.discovery.com/science/Double-Slit-Experiment.
3. "The Uncertainty Principle: Way down at the quantum scale, one thing you can be absolutely sure of is uncertainty." Quantumatlas.umd.edu, The Quantum Atlas, Retrieved August 30, 2023. https://quantumatlas.umd.edu/entry/uncertainty-principle/.
4. "How hard is it to win the lottery? Odds to keep in mind as Powerball and Mega Millions jackpots soar." APNews.com, Associated Press News, July 19, 2023. https://apnews.com/article/powerball-mega-millions-winning-odds-numbers-a3e5a8e8e7ed15d7500c1d6acdab6785.

5. Attention and the Power of Focus

1. Gloria Mark, "Speaking of Psychology: Why our attention spans are shrinking," *American Psychological Association*, last modified February 2023, https://www.apa.org/news/podcasts/speaking-of-psychology/attention-spans.
2. Each person's journey is different. How I follow the Way, or Christ, will be different from yours. What life brings me will be different than what it brings you. Your purpose for being here will manifest itself in time, as will mine, and it will be different from mine. Just as Jesus had a purpose and meaning for His life, so do you. Our focus should be the Way, how He lived His life, which was always love; love above everything.

3. From a sermon by Manley Beasley (1931-1990), a spiritual mystic and teacher.
4. "Meditation" Wikipedia, accessed December 28, 2023. https://en.wikipedia.org/wiki/Meditation.

6. Intention, Imagination, and Vision

1. Henry Miller. *Tropic of Cancer* (Mansfield Centre: Martino Publishing, 2015).
2. Jakab, Peter. "Leonardo da Vinci and Flight." Smithsonian National Air and Space Museum, accessed April 6, 2025, https://airandspace.si.edu/stories/editorial/leonardo-da-vinci-and-flight.
3. "History of the Cylinder Phonograph," Library of Congress, accessed April 6, 2025, https://www.loc.gov/collections/edison-company-motion-pictures-and-sound-recordings/articles-and-essays/history-of-edison-sound-recordings/history-of-the-cylinder-phonograph/.
4. Browne, Ryan. "From AI assistants to Big Tech breakup: World Wide Web inventor's top predictions as it turns 35," CNBC.com, accessed April 6, 2025, https://www.cnbc.com/2024/03/12/world-wide-web-turns-35-tim-berners-lee-gives-predictions-for-future.html.

7. The High Energy of Gratitude

1. Sperry, Roger W., Gazzaniga, Michael S., and Bogen, Joseph E. "Interhemispheric Relationships: The Neocortical Commissures; Syndromes of Hemisphere Disconnection." In Handbook of Clinical Neurology, edited by P. J. Vinken and G.W. Bruyn, vol. 4, 273-290. Amsterdam: North-Holland, 1969.
2. Chowdhury, Madhuleena. "The Neuroscience of Gratitude and Effects on the Brain." Positive Psychology, April 9, 2019. https://positivepsychology.com/neuroscience-of-gratitude/.
3. Lisa Barrett, *How Emotions Are Made* (Boston: Mariner Books, 2018).
4. Veazey, Karen "Why Emotional Self-regulation Is Important And How To Do It," Medical News Today, May 3, 2022, https://www.medicalnewstoday.com/articles/emotional-self-regulation.

8. The Power of Thoughts and Words

1. Vance, Erik. *Suggestible You: The Curious Science Of Your Brain's Ability To Deceive, Transform, And Heal* (Washington D.C.: National Geographic, 2016) 24.
2. Joe Dispenza. *You Are The Placebo: Making Your Mind Matter* (Carlsbad: Hay House USA, 2014), 128-129.
3. Brown, Kirk; Creswell, David; Greco, Carol; Dutcher, Janine; Lindsay, Emily; Marsland, Anna; Stern, Harrison; Walko, Thomas; Wright, Aidan. "Mindfulness-based stress reduction increases stimulated IL-6 production among lonely older adults: A randomized controlled trial." Science Direct, Volume 104, August 2022. https://www.sciencedirect.com/science/article/abs/pii/S0889159122001258.

4. Gowin, Joshua. "Brain Scans Show How Meditation Improves Mental Focus: Meditators have stable brains and stable thoughts." Psychology Today, April 20, 2012. https://www.psychologytoday.com/us/blog/you-illuminated/201204/brain-scans-show-how-meditation-improves-mental-focus.
5. Powell, Alvin. "More mindfulness may be part of the answer for anxiety-ridden U.S." Harvard Gazette, February 1, 2023. https://news.harvard.edu/gazette/story/2023/02/can-mindfulness-help-anxiety-trial-suggests-yes.
6. Rutledge, Thomas. "How Meditation Improves Emotional and Physical Health." Psychology Today, August 4, 2019. https://www.psychologytoday.com/us/blog/the-healthy-journey/201908/how-meditation-improves-emotional-and-physical-health.
7. Neale, Miles. "The Guide To Mindfulness Meditation: How and Why Mindfulness Can Help." Anxiety.org, March 1, 2024. https://insighttimer.com/milesneale/guided-meditations/guidelines-for-mindfulness-practice.
8. Joe Dispenza, *Breaking The Habit Of Being Yourself: How To Lose Your Mind And Create A New One* (Carlsbad: Hay House, Inc., 2012), 177-178.

9. Manifesting in the Five Percent

1. Coleman Barks and John Moyne, translators, *The Essential Rumi* (San Francisco: HarperOne, 2004).
2. Abraham Isaac Kook, *Orot HaKodesh*. Vol. 3 (Mossad Harav Kook, 1985) 324.
3. Nag Hamadi Library, Gospel Of Thomas, Text 77.

10. Everything You Need Is Within You

1. Homeostasis is the process by which your body keeps everything in balance, like temperature, fluid levels, and energy, to stay in a stable, healthy state. It works automatically to adjust when things change outside or inside your body. For example, if you get too hot, your body sweats to cool you down; if you get too cold, you shiver to warm up. Essentially, homeostasis helps your body stay on track and function properly, even when conditions around you change.

11. Living from Within

1. Miller, Kori. "Using Self-Awareness Theory and Skills in Psychology." Positive Psychology, January 7, 2020. https://positivepsychology.com/self-awareness-theory-skills/.
2. Daniel Goleman, *Emotional Intelligence* (New York: Bantam Books, 2005) 43. Goleman's definition of emotional intelligence is focused on emotional awareness, but his explanation helps us understand what we mean by being aware of our spiritual reality.

Appendix Three: Affirmations

1. Dimas, Jessica, "Do Affirmations Really Work?" Dwell in Magic, September 9, 2023. https://jessicadimas.com/87-positive-i-am-affirmations-for-success-self-love-healing/#I_AM_Affirmations_for_Self-Love.

Acknowledgments

I'm grateful to all the scientists in the fields of quantum mechanics, astronomy, cosmology, anthropology, geology, archeology, physics, medicine, psychology and biology for their contributions to my education and maturation from religion to genuine authentic spirituality and learning to embrace general revelation.

I'm grateful to Steve McVey for his help in understanding the process of manifesting in the 95 percent.

Thanks to TWS Publishing and Robin Smit who supervised the editing and publishing of the book and to Carrie Scott who did the editing.

Thanks to my clients over the years who have allowed me to hone these truths in my spiritual coaching practice.

Thanks to my wife Cyndi who edited the book as I wrote it and gave creative feedback.

Thanks to Dolores Cannon who helped me see that being a light worker is the greatest calling I could have.

About the Author

D. Scott Cook is a former senior pastor and the founder and president of Abiding in Agape, a spiritual coaching and teaching nonprofit dedicated to helping people make peace with their past, transition from controlling religion to a spirituality they can embrace, and learn to thrive, not just survive.

He hosts the weekly international broadcast program Breaking Free From Churchianity on the Grace Awakening Network and gantv.com. It's also a podcast on your favorite podcast directory or RSS.com.

He's also the author of *Breaking Free From Churchianity: How to Live Free From Religious Legalism, Destructive Church Dogma, and People-Pleasing in Churches* and *Alignment of Authentic Love: Living Your Highest Life,* both available on Amazon in hardback, paperback and eBook.

Scott has over thirty years of experience in pastoral ministry, spiritual coaching, and business/professional training and coaching. He graduated from Oklahoma State University with a Bachelor of Science in

Business and from Southwestern Baptist Theological Seminary with a Master of Divinity in Biblical Languages. He has also taught in leadership seminars, professional training classes, churches, retreats, and conferences throughout the United States and other parts of the world.

Scott and his wife Cyndi live in the Dallas area of Texas. He is the father of two adult boys and is also a grandfather.

Other Books by D. Scott Cook

Breaking Free From Churchianity is an enlightening guide to rediscovering faith through the lens of God's unconditional love and grace, untethered by the constraints of traditional denominational religion. Join the journey beyond dogma to a place where the love of God and Jesus Christ is the sole foundation of belief.

Learn to be free from:

- The burden of religious legalism.
- Destructive church dogma.
- The unending cycle of people-pleasing in churches.
- And more!

Alignment of Authentic Love: Living Your Highest Life takes you on an amazing journey to know God's true nature and identity so you can know your true nature and identity. Why? Because until you do, you can't love and enjoy yourself, have healthy relationships with others, or a relationship of love and trust with the Source of all life. Your very reason for living!

Learn how to:

- Enjoy a dynamic relationship with a loving God.
- Come to terms with past trauma to embrace and love yourself.
- Be free emotionally to have healthy, loving relationships with others.
- Release anxieties and worries to enjoy mental, emotional, and spiritual peace and rest.
- And more!

Discover more from TWS Publishing—our authors, their books, and our growing collection of co-authored works rooted in grace and truth.

www.thewriterssocietypublishing.com

www.ingramcontent.com/pod-product-compliance
Lightning Source LLC
Chambersburg PA
CBHW070447050426
42451CB00015B/3373